DEAN GRIESS

Don't Show Your Duckbutt

Tools to Kick A$$ in Front of Any Audience

First published by 122Hibiscus Publishing 2024

Copyright © 2024 by Dean Griess

All rights reserved. No part of this publication may be reproduced, stored or transmitted in any form or by any means, electronic, mechanical, photocopying, recording, scanning, or otherwise without written permission from the publisher. It is illegal to copy this book, post it to a website, or distribute it by any other means without permission.

Dean Griess asserts the moral right to be identified as the author of this work.

Designations used by companies to distinguish their products are often claimed as trademarks. All brand names and product names used in this book and on its cover are trade names, service marks, trademarks and registered trademarks of their respective owners. The publishers and the book are not associated with any product or vendor mentioned in this book. None of the companies referenced within the book have endorsed the book.

First edition

ISBN: 979-8-218-53613-8

This book was professionally typeset on Reedsy.
Find out more at reedsy.com

This book is dedicated to my family.

Ramsey and Ryker, you push me to be better daily. Sandra, I would not be who I am without your love and support.

I love you!

Contents

Foreword iv

I Setting the Foundation

1 Presenter vs Facilitator 3
2 Training/Presenting the Art Form 4
    It is a Superpower 5
3 3 P's – Poise, Personality, Persistence 7
    Poise 7
    Personality 8
    Persistence 8
4 What It Takes to be Great 11
    Authenticity 12
    Confidence 14
    Preparation 15
    Audience Experience 17
    Delivery Success Equation 19

II Tools of the Trade

5 AUTHENTICITY 25
    Movement 25
    Voice 30
    Word Choice 43
    Gestures 45
    Eye Contact 53

6	CONFIDENCE	57
	Presence	57
	Humor	64
	Being Present	67
	Nervous Habits	69
	Overcoming Nervous Habits	79
	Appearance	84
7	PREPARATION	90
	Self	90
	Refocus Your Mind	101
	Materials	104
	Technology	113
	What Preparation Does for You	119
	Room Setup	120
	Organize the Room	123
	Preparation Sequence	131
	Dean's Preparation Sequence	133
8	AUDIENCE EXPERIENCE	141
	Focus on the Experience	142
	Avoid Narrating Your Actions	144
	Empathy Mindset	145
	Understand Their Business.	146
	Impactful Openings	153
	DAGR Best Practices	158
	Activity Cycle	161
	Question Types	172
	Tackling Questions Process	176
	Power Closings	184
	Reading the Room	193

III	Success & Responsibility	
9	Delivery Success	203
10	Transferable Skills	210
11	Grow, Pursue, Pass on	219
	Growing Your Skills	219
	Pursue Unattainable Perfection	226
	Pass On	229
12	Wrap Up	232

Appendix	234
Cheat Codes	234

Foreword

Take a moment. Close your eyes. In your mind, think of a duck floating across a pond. What do you see?

Smooth. Calm. Effortless.

Now take a moment and picture the same duck as he attempts to grab food from under the surface of the water. What do you see?

Splashes. Feet chaotically kicking. Butt in the air.

This is a metaphor for the life of a trainer or presenter. When things are going well, there is an air of smoothness. A level of calm confidence. It looks effortless.

Yet, when things get off track like when technology doesn't work, forget what comes next, receive a tough question. That's when the splashing starts. "Chaotic kicking" begins to show on the face. Stumbling over words.

This is also known as showing your "duck butt."

This book is designed to establish a framework of tools that anyone can deploy in front of an audience to maintain a cool, calm demeanor that creates a quality experience for those in attendance.

I have seen folks have negative physical reactions to being in front of an audience. It is tough to watch because I could see the trembling terror that has overridden their personal operating system. My heart breaks for them.

That is why I am writing this book. I want to equip others with the tools and practices that help tackle this fear and kick ass in front of any audience.

I've been facilitating and presenting for over 20 years. I've dedicated 10,000+ hours honing my craft and coached or trained over 1,000 facilitators/presenters. My unbridled passion for creating exceptional experiences and helping others do the same is my career obsession.

One thing you will notice there is not just ONE way to be successful in front of an audience. The intent is to equip you with tools and concepts that have proven effective for not only myself but others I've worked with.

I

Setting the Foundation

1

Presenter vs Facilitator

In this book, the terms *Facilitators* and *Presenters* will be used frequently. Although similar, presenting and facilitating are two distinct skill-sets.

Being a great presenter doesn't necessarily mean being a great facilitator, and vice versa. However, it is entirely possible to excel at both.

Definitions:

- **Presenting** is the ability to engage an audience by "pushing" content through one-way communication (e.g., conveying knowledge).
- **Facilitating** is the ability to engage an audience through a "give-and-take" form of two-way communication (e.g., interacting and "pulling" content from an audience).

Regardless of your current situation, you have likely acted as a presenter or facilitator. For instance, managers in a call center can play both roles. They may have to train their staff on a new concept or refresh a skill on current desired skill. They may have to present to their entire team in team huddles. You don't have to have the official title of presenter or facilitator in order to operate in either of these capacities.

2

Training/Presenting the Art Form

The most talented presenters and facilitators can breathe life into any content.

Regardless of how bland the material may be, a skilled facilitator can create a captivating experience for an audience. Conversely, even beautifully created content, if delivered by an unskilled or unconfident facilitator, won't have the desired impact. This is the ability to take an audience on a journey that enhances knowledge and skills while leaving a lasting impression.

Those that are great can make it look effortless, but what is not seen is the work and effort that gets put into the craft (below the water for ducks).

The tireless preparation, the replaying events over and over, the accepting of audience feedback, receiving coaching, balancing time, focusing on achieving objectives, disconnecting from outside distractions, staying in the moment, being technologically adept, remaining adaptable to unforeseen circumstances, trying new techniques, balancing difficult interactions, soaking in knowledge to hone the craft. All of that can be just for one event, which adds up over hundreds of classes and events.

It is a Superpower

The power to move people through the use of your voice and actions is a skill that carries tremendous upside.

This superpower can be utilized in any professional role:

- Leading Meetings
- Proposing an Idea
- Waiting Tables
- Asking for a Raise
- Collaborating with Colleagues

At its core, it is effective communication while confidently presenting yourself.

The power to move people starts with finding your *voice*. The search for your voice starts with having the confidence to use the talent you possess, but in front of an audience.

Think about when you are having a conversation with your closest friend. I'd venture to guess that you have no problem finding your "voice" (e.g. speaking confidently). This can be one of the hardest transitions for many. Throughout the classes I have trained for presenters or facilitators, I have seen countless people struggle with transitioning from being a contributing member of the class to being in front of the same group and presenting a topic. There is a fear that overrides their capability to use their *voice*.

The great news is there have been pillars in the business community that mention the ability to speak publicly is the one of the most powerful skill-sets to harness. Those pillars being Warren Buffet, Charles Schwab (finance), and Dale Carnegie.

There is a stigma amongst people that presenting or facilitating is the worst thing in the world they could be asked to do. *Why?*

- Being the Focus of Attention?
- Fear of Being Judged?
- Fear of Being Ridiculed?
- Feeling Vulnerable?
- Exposed to an Attack?

Every single person in the world has the ability to be great in front of an audience. Just like with any skill, some may have an easier time adapting to it while others have to work REALLY hard at it.

It is a similar scenario with professional athletes. Kids dream of growing up to play in the NFL, MLB, NHL, Premier Futbol League, or the NBA. Some of these kids have the wonderful combination of natural ability and physical structure that creates great opportunities.

They also possess an insane work ethic that complements their physical gifts.

Yes, professional athletes have natural abilities to run, jump, throw, skate, etc. BUT the ability to communicate to other humans is something that is ingrained in each and every one of us.

If you truly want to be better at speaking publicly, you can be. If you tell yourself, you'll never be good at it, or you are too afraid, guess what... you will never be able to do it.

You need to be committed and believe you can be great before you can be.

3

3 P's - Poise, Personality, Persistence

To prepare you for your journey to create exceptional experiences for audiences, it is important to understand the bedrock for greatness. These three elements are the foundation for what it takes to be great in front of any audience.

Poise

Think back to our duck on the pond.

Regardless of what is going on under the surface, maintaining your poise is paramount to your success. If something doesn't go right (e.g. technology breakdown), act as if it were supposed to happen. Perhaps make a joke at the situation. If the projector stops working in the middle of the class, you can say, "I guess the internet gremlins are trying to prevent us from completing our session." One of my favorite go-to phrases to make light of a technology issue is "internet gremlins."

Personality

When people first start out in presenting or facilitating, they try WAY too hard to be something they are not. When facilitating trainer preparatory or certification classes, I have seen a wide range of these instances. I've seen people try to change their voice to sound like a 90s radio disc jockey. They over-exaggerate gestures. They try to avoid using their hands. The biggest problem is this is not who they are. Those that can be themselves and demonstrate their awesome personality are the ones that resonate most with audiences.

"Always Be You!" is the phrase I pulled from the movie Central Intelligence. In the movie, Dwayne "The Rock" Johnson is a spy who has a very quirky personality and in one of the earlier scenes, he wears a light blue shirt with a cartoon unicorn. Underneath the unicorn it reads, "Always Be You." I actually purchased the shirt because I loved the message it conveys, especially as it pertains to the skill of speaking in public. This is one of my favorite shirts that I've purchased. It has also been a fun social experiment to wear this shirt through airports. Being a larger individual (6'4" and 235 lbs), it is fun to see the reactions of others, but I digress.

Although the shirt is quirky by itself, the message is appropriate for any facilitator or presenter. You have a unique personality. You have something to offer an audience. When in front of an audience, it is important to let your audience embrace your uniqueness.

Persistence

There will be times when you will feel defeated. A class doesn't go as planned, possibly a series of classes, you need to stay focused. Identify where mishaps may have occurred.

1. Was it a class dynamic?
2. Do you need to build better rapport?
3. Were there misses in the content or objectives?

Whatever the cause... OWN IT, FIX IT, MOVE ON!

There are times you may need to go back to your inspiration of why you want to be exceptional presenting or facilitating. Your inspiration could be anything, but it will be unique to you. Revisiting that motivation can be what keeps you moving forward toward your goal of being great.

Your inspiration could be the fact that you were moved by a particularly exceptional presenter or facilitator, and you thought, "I want to do that." If that is the case, you may need to go back and watch their videos.

For me, I draw inspiration from a variety of sources. I have seen greatness in a classroom (more on that later) and I have been inspired by great speakers. Three of the best speakers that I have watched repeatedly are Tony Robbins, Simon Sinek, and Dan Pink. All three of them, not only have great messages, but they are true to themselves and can move an audience. When I have hit those low points, I watch their videos.

It is important to know, the difference between those that are great and those that are not, is the great ones never gave up.

If you haven't noticed, I love movies. There are so many great messages that can be extracted from movies. When it comes to persistence, there is none better than the movie *The Founder*.

In the movie, Michael Keaton plays Ray Kroc, who made McDonald's into the global conglomerate in which we are familiar. During a portion of the movie, he delivers a monologue while he is preparing to deliver a speech about persistence:

> *"Now, I know what you're thinkin'. How the hell does a 52-year-old, over-the-hill milkshake machine salesman... build a fast-food empire with 16,000 restaurants, in 50 states, in 5 foreign countries... with an annual revenue of in the neighborhood of $700,000,000.00... One word... PERSISTENCE.*
>
> *Nothing in this world can take the place of good old persistence. Talent won't. Nothing's more common than unsuccessful men with talent. Genius won't. Unrecognized genius is practically a cliche. Education won't. Why the world is full of educated fools. Persistence and determination alone are all powerful."*

There will be situations where you are working on a particular skill to be a great speaker and it feels like it is taking forever. Stay the course, it will happen for you.

4

What It Takes to be Great

I fell into a trap.

I had gone through the formative years of my life (elementary through high school), through college, and even early in my adult work-life never realizing the individuals I observed in front of classes and audiences had to work to get to that point. They found a way to connect with their classes and leave a lasting impact. When I started this journey to write this book, I've reflected a lot on those that have stood out to me.

One of which was my middle-school science teacher, Mr. Maxim. This dude was quirky and loved science. He also found ways to connect with the awkward aged middle-schoolers. His passion for science was evident, yet he never missed an opportunity to keep things silly. Two examples I still remember vividly, even 30+ years later.

While explaining certain science physics theories, he demonstrated it by doing a standing jump onto his desk. That took the entire class by surprise, which kept us interested. He also knew when we needed a brain break for being silly. One day, a classmate fell asleep in class, which he was prone to do. On this particular occasion, he whispered instructions to the entire class to gather their things, and move to the hallway.

He then climbed up and advanced the clock to read 6:00pm.

He nonchalantly went over to the desk of the sleeping student to wake him up. He told him he was not sure what happened, but he'd been sleeping, and it was now 6:00pm. The bewilderment that showed across the slumbering students face was hysterical while twenty or more of us giggled in the hallway.

Although I fell into this trap before truly realizing the effort and skill it takes to move a class or audience, they are lessons I reflect fondly upon because of the impact they had on me.

Due to examples, like the one above, along with a career dedicated to this art form, I have concluded that the ability to be great in front of an audience comes down to four things: *Authenticity*, *Confidence*, *Preparation*, and *Audience Experience*.

Authenticity

The concept of authenticity is usually one of the harder components for anyone new to the profession of speaking in public and can also be tough for those more tenured. For our purposes, the definition of authenticity is the ability to be true to oneself.

This is the ability to be comfortable in your own skin and how you communicate. There have been many instances where newer presenters will attempt to be something they are not. Whether you believe it or not, people in an audience have highly attuned "BS Meters." These are the meters that can tell if someone is trying to bullshit (BS) them. It is that feeling when you are walking through a store and you are approached by a salesperson and you can tell the person has no interest in helping you find what you want and only focused on pushing a particular product. The same applies in the realm of presentation. Audiences will get the feeling, the person in front of them is trying too hard.

In being true to yourself in front of an audience, the great ones have the ability to balance between their true personality and the audience dynamics. The value of finding this balance is the ability to authentically connect with an audience. An example of this might be if you are a direct communicator (e.g. no fluff and straightforward style, everything is very black and white) and your audience may be a little more emotionally centered, this may not mix well.

You may see this if you love to tell stories in front of an audience to help support a point. In doing so, you utilize a lot of "flowery" language (e.g. elaboration). If you have an audience of system engineers whose jobs are very binary, there is a high likelihood that the audience could become disconnected with your stories, because that does not fit into their communication style preference. We dive deeper into how to adapt your authenticity when we get to *Audience Experience* (Chapter 8).

Understanding who you are is the place you want to start.

- Are you super friendly?
- Are you direct in your communication?
- Are you a hugger?
- Are you a non-toucher (prefer big personal bubble)?
- Are you the type of person that likes to keep work and personal lives separate?
- Are you an introvert?
- Are you an extrovert?

These are just some of the questions that you can ask yourself to better understand your true authentic self.

Your ability to be authentic can be developed through utilizing five key components. Those components are:

- Movement
- Voice
- Word Choice
- Gestures
- Eye Contact

We explore these five areas more in the *Authenticity* chapter.

Confidence

Confidence is the feeling that you can accomplish anything. In essence, confidence is the feeling of being comfortable in your own skin. Although on the surface, authenticity and confidence seem very similar, there is a difference, especially in regard to how you show up for your audience.

Confidence is something I grew up struggling with. My tendency was to blend into the environment around me, not be noticed, and be just another face. This was highlighted in the late-2000s when I went through the Personality Index course. I remember explicitly the trainer looking at my results and telling me, "You are a chameleon." I was speechless, this was the most accurate assessment I'd ever had to that point. It was 100% accurate. I spent most of my life up to that point blending into whatever group I was a part of. This was exemplified when I was in high school. Although I had groups in which I was a part, I was able to get along with anyone rather easily, however it was usually through adapting to the dynamic of the group or primarily being a silent observer and not making "waves."

Even though I've grown more into my personality throughout my career, I have realized that "chameleon" nature served me well when training classes. I felt confident adapting to situations and varying class dynamics, which ultimately led to increased confidence for me.

Even if you are not a natural chameleon, you can still have great confidence. Yet, depending on the strength of your personality, you need to understand that adapting to varying audience dynamics may be a struggle.

Your ability to display confidence can be developed through utilizing five key components. Those components are:

- Presence
- Humor
- Being present
- Nervous habits
- Appearance

Preparation

Preparation is an area that gets overlooked easily as it is the area that most don't see. This is what happens behind the curtain.

If you've seen the movie, *The Wizard of Oz*, when Dorothy and her travel companions finally make it to Oz to see the wizard so Dorothy can find her way back to Kansas. They are ushered into a huge, cavernous room and what they see is a lot of smoke and what appears to be a large mythical type of being with a booming voice. This is what is perceived to be the wizard. As the wizard begins calling each of them and firing edicts of how they should proceed to obtain what they desire most, Toto (Dorothy's little dog) becomes highly curious and locates a little man behind a curtain that is pulling various levers and shouting into a microphone type of device. Shortly after Toto begins pulling the curtain, the mythical type being with his booming voice says:

"PAY NO ATTENTION TO THE MAN BEHIND THE CURTAIN!"

SPOILER ALERT... Come to find out, the man behind the curtain was actually the wizard but took a great deal of effort to craft his persona of the all-knowing Oz.

I mention this movie not to go against what was mentioned about Authenticity and not being true to who you are, but to call out the amount of preparation it took the actual wizard to create this persona. That level of preparation is what it took to create the desired experience for those wanting to visit the "All powerful Oz."

When you have attended a well delivered training class or engaging presentation, you have experienced what the presenter/facilitator intended you to have.

There are countless hours that go into preparing for a successful experience. If done right, the most minute details do not get overlooked. It can be as big as technology testing all the way down to pen placement for each audience member.

When preparing for a class or speaking event, no stone should be left unturned.

There should be core questions you should ask yourself:

- What do you need to do to be prepared personally?
- Do you know your objectives for what your want to achieve with your session?
- Have you adequately reviewed your content?

- What else needs to be considered to enhance the audience experience?

The tools needed to ensure your success in answering the above questions are:

- Self-preparation
- Refocus your mind
- Materials
- Technology
- Room set-up
- Preparation sequence

Audience Experience

The audience experience is the one of the biggest elements that anyone speaking in public should be focused on. Far too often, those I've worked with get caught up in worrying about what they are doing and lose sight of the audience. With the countless observations I have conducted, there is a visible instance when someone really gets off track because there is a sense of panic that shows up on the face of the speaker. This is because they are worried about covering all the applicable speaking points or worried about how they are showing up. You can actually see the speaker begin to audit the "checklist" in their brain. That is when "panic eyes" are plastered all over the face.

There are core questions you should ask yourself when considering the audience experience:

- What does the audience/class need?
- What is the value you are delivering?

- What is the culture of the company/team/audience?
- Was the session adapted to meet all attendees (e.g. blended learning modalities)?
- Were stories utilized?
- Did they enjoy the time with you?

These questions are a great starting point and can also be effective questions to ask when your talents are requested to deliver a session and how you may construct/adapt your delivery.

Once you have insights into the questions above, these are the tools to ensure you are able to meet the audience where they are:

- Focus on Experience
- Impactful Openings
- Activity Cycle
- Question Types
- Tackling Questions
- Power Closings
- Reading the Room

All four of these areas can lead you to your ultimate goal, Delivery Success. This is the sweet spot for any presentation/training. This means you've successfully met the objectives of the session. The audience has actionable takeaways that can applied as soon as they walk out the door. Most importantly, your session will be memorable. If you have learners or audience members walking out of your session saying, "This is the best training/presentation I've ever attended," you know you've hit the mark.

Delivery Success Equation

The idea of *Delivery Success* can be ambiguous. Then if you couple that with the fact everyone will have a perspective as to what goes into a successful session. And to throw the most epic monkey wrench into things, there is not a consistent way to answer the age-old "If, then" question as it pertains to our art form: "If I do this, then it will lead my success in front of an audience."

To help in the enhancement of your ability as a trainer/presenter, I've created an equation to help you answer this question using the four areas previously mentioned.

Delivery Success Equation - $Ds = Ax(A,C,P)$

- Ds-Delivery Success
- Ax-Audience Experience
- A-Authenticity
- C-Confidence
- P-Preparation

Let's unpack this.

If we start with the elements within the parenthesis (*Authenticity*, *Confidence*, and *Preparation*), all three of these elements comprise our behaviors when we are in front of an audience. It is how we show up as our true selves (*Authenticity*), how our audience perceives us (*Confidence*), and how we ensure we are putting ourselves in the best possible position to succeed (*Preparation*).

When we can truly assess our commitment and willingness to continuously grow in these spaces, then we shift to the tactical skills attributed to mindset for any session (*Audience Experience*).

The *Audience Experience* is the mindset commitment that is enhanced through tactical skills that create a better overall experience for our audiences.

Delivery Success is our ultimate goal for any time we are in front of an audience. In order to achieve success, the four areas outlined in the book help get us to that point.

The goal of any session is to achieve *Delivery Success*. Which I have found to be a culmination of the four key areas.

Using an observation form, you will have the opportunity to score yourself accordingly and to enhance your skills. This form can also be utilized by someone familiar with these skills.

Quick precautionary note, be sure if you ask someone to observe you, it is important they are familiar with the skills and tactics from this book. I have seen too many individuals get frustrated by the feedback received from an observer who is unfamiliar with items contained on an observation form. This usually stems from perceiving a concept one way versus the intended purpose (e.g. asking questions vs. asking the right type of questions) or uncertainty of process (e.g. tackling questions).

The key to growing your skills to create exceptional experiences for audiences is honesty. If you are scoring yourself, whether from memory or watching a recording, you need to be brutally honest with yourself. This level of honesty is where growth happens. Just because I mention brutal honesty, it is not to only focus on the growth opportunities, you will want to be honest with your successes as well. You can also ask for brutal honesty from your observers as well.

The feedback is focused on the skills demonstrated; it is not an attack on who you are as a person. It may feel like that, just continue to remind yourself, "this is how I get better."

The intent with this equation is to afford you the opportunity to quantify your growth as a trainer/presenter.

Now that we've established the foundation for the four areas and how you can evaluate your growth, let's start reviewing each of the four areas and how you can kick ass in front of your audiences.

II

Tools of the Trade

5

AUTHENTICITY

Movement

Facilitators and presenters are like pick-pockets. If you think about the skill it takes to be a successful pick pocket, the elements that work to their benefit is they utilize the art of misdirection and distraction to avoid your ability to focus on what they are focusing on.

The TedTalk by Apollo Robbins is one of my all-time favorites. In his talk, he references how our brains are wired and there is only so much we can focus on at any given time. During his talk, he brings an audience member up on stage and while he utilizes his words and different touch points, Apollo has the audience member focusing on what he WANTS him to focus on versus where he is focusing. For instance, at one point, Apollo engages the audience member by holding onto his wrist and then casually shifts the focus of the unsuspecting "mark" to his pant leg and various other points of his body.

This is all while Apollo has never surrendered the grasp of the audience members wrist. During these various distractions, Apollo nonchalantly unfastens the watch band and takes his watch. He eventually gives the watch back to the audience member.

As facilitators and presenters, we have a very similar power at our disposal, and it starts with our movement. We have the capability to control where our audience looks and how they engage based on where we position ourselves.

Too many times, I have seen facilitators, especially, cripple themselves because they feel they have to be in the front of the room. This internal belief is absolutely wrong.

There are four areas that can be utilized to your advantage:

- In front of the audience
- To the side of the audience
- Behind the audience
- Visualize key points

In front of the audience

When you are in front of the room, this puts you in the position to be the primary focus. Ideally, this is where you will be the center of attention. This is the best spot when you are welcoming the audience (e.g. starting a session), conducting introductions, and facilitating discussions.

To the side of the audience

By moving to the side of the audience, this shifts the perspective and depending on where you want them to focus, you remain in the peripheral view of the audience. This space is great when you want the audience to have their primary focus on the slides you are using, but you remain in the indirect view of the audience to compliment what they may be viewing.

Behind the audience

This can be a scary place for presenters and facilitators in which to move. It goes against the limiting belief mentioned previously. However, there is a great deal of power that comes from being comfortable moving into this area. When you are in this area, you can draw the attention away from you and make the full focus be on the media (e.g. PowerPoint). The other added benefit that comes from this is audience members need a shift in perspective and/or need to move a little more to keep them focused. Keep in mind, this one may not be as utilized for presenters depending on the room set up. If you are on a stage in front of hundreds, this may not be an option. Use your best judgement.

Visualize Key Points

Although it is not necessarily a part of the room in which to move, your movement can be utilized add a visual component to key points. For instance, if you are reviewing a sequence of steps your learners need to understand, you can physically move your body to different points in a line as you progress through each point. This can aid in the knowledge retention of your learners by adding the visual element to your content.

Movement is truly that simple. These four types of movement put you in a strong position to control the view of your audience and how you engage them.

Knowing the areas in which we can move, there are some things that are important in which to be mindful of as you move.

Be aware of the space

Not every space is created equal. Some rooms are huge. Some rooms are small. Some rooms are short. Some rooms are tall. Once you begin filling it with an audience and the applicable tables and chairs, it will change the dynamics of the room. The tip I have provided facilitators and presenters is, **don't work for the room, make the room work for you.** This means that you need to ensure you have the ability to use the space to your advantage.

By making the room work for you, you need to ensure you have the ability to successfully navigate throughout the room. One of the biggest "watchouts" is identifying tripping hazards. This primary culprit of tripping even the best of presenters and facilitators is power cords. If these trip hazards are not identified ahead of time, one of two things will occur. You will either bite the dust in front of your audience OR if you are lucky enough to prevent your fall, you will likely disconnect your technology (e.g. projector).

As you identify the potential "watchouts" in the space would be working in, it is important to know where you can maneuver. One area that has served me well is knowing the paths that I can take throughout the session. Am I able to move successfully to each part of the room? Is there enough space for me to move to reinforce key points?

With the answers to these questions, it is important to account for the audience once they arrive. This includes planning for chairs not being pushed into the tables, laptop bags, and various other personal sundries.

IMPORTANT: Make sure you know where you can walk so you don't walk through the projector light.

This particular point has been contentious with presenters/facilitators I've worked with. It has been refuted that it is necessary to point out key points, especially in system demos. How I look at this is you are putting yourself in a distraction risk by "dancing" in the projector light.

This showed up during a session I was observing a lady was doing an Excel demo for the class. She was doing well by positioning herself in a seated position to the left side of the screen and still able to see the screen and the audience.

HOWEVER, what she didn't account for was what was waiting for her in the lower left-hand corner of the old windows versions. If you are familiar with the older versions of Windows, think about what used to be located in the lower left-hand corner of the screen. That's right! The START button. Needless to say, every time she turned to face the audience, she had START plastered across her forehead. It was as silly and awkward as you'd imagine.

The same applies with shapes that are included on PowerPoint slides. If you walk into the projector light to point something out, there is a high likelihood that you may have an arrow pointing at a part of your body you would prefer not to be pointed at.

Movement's Enemy

You guessed it, successful movement has an enemy. This enemy is also something that many presenters and facilitators love and have a hard time disconnecting from. That enemy is the infamous podium.

Whenever a podium is present, it attracts presenters and facilitators like a moth to a flame. It is a comfort device and completely disconnects the speaker from the audience. Ultimately it creates a barrier between the two parties.

Don't get me wrong, I have used podiums before but only for connecting my laptop to the overhead and/or a place to place my notes/guides. Those are the only times you should be visiting the podium, the rest of the time you should be moving throughout the room and connecting with your audience.

The most unique situation I ever encountered observing a facilitator that loved the podium was when I was working for a call center outsourcing company. We had a tv and camera set up in the room so I could observe virtually (this was years before Zoom was a thing). During the first day of observations, the trainer never moved away from the podium because he wanted to have his Facilitator Guide close by. Over the next few hours, the only time he moved his feet away from the podium was when it was break time. After that first day, I met with him and mentioned he needed to move throughout the room to better engage his class.

Well, I got what I asked for. The next day, he started his class at the podium and began facilitating, then the unthinkable happened, he took the podium with him. The trainer began moving throughout the room while pushing the podium in front of him. It became even more awkward because it was not a small podium and the space between the learners was somewhat narrow, so the participants had to move out of his way for the next few hours.

Technically, this particular trainer followed my instructions, and it was a lessoned learned for me. Be much more specific on how to move by taking a few pages of notes with him throughout the room, and not the podium.

Movement is important and yet whenever you move, it has to be purposeful. Don't move just for the sake of moving.

Voice

As a presenter/facilitator, our voice is our most powerful attribute. Let's be honest, how many effective speakers have you seen deliver a quality experience without their voice. If you have, that would be a session, I'd love to attend.

This is the tool we utilize to communicate a message, tell a story, inspire the masses, move people to action. Knowing how to utilize your voice can enhance your ability to achieve all of the aforementioned goals.

There are five elements for utilizing an effective voice:

- Efficient Breathing
- Confident tone
- Articulation
- Dynamic
- Projection

Efficient Breathing

In order to use our voice, we need air in our lungs. We have all been exchanging oxygen and carbon dioxide ever since each of us have entered the world. It is something on a daily basis, we don't think much about. Yet, when we get in front of an audience, we need more of it, then depending on the level of nervousness, we can't get enough of it.

Having the ability to be efficient with our ability to exchange oxygen and carbon dioxide could be the difference between having plenty of air, stressing out because we can't find enough.

The concept of efficient breathing is the ability to fill your lungs in the shortest amount of time possible. This does not mean taking really short breaths. All that will do is force you into a tightened state. As you tighten up, you breathe faster, you become more nervous, and quite possibly become lightheaded. The last thing I want you to do is to pass out in front of your audience.

To better understand how to efficiently breathe, I want you to try a couple things first:

Take a moment, take a full, deep breath in through your nose. This likely felt quite good and relaxing, which is great.

Now, I want you to do the exact same thing, but this time, I want you to take another deep breath but only inhale through your mouth.

Did you feel the difference?

Both of these are effective ways to breathe, however neither are the most efficient.

I want to share a trick I learned when I was in band in high school. To paint the picture, when I was in high school, I played the Tuba. This is the big brass instrument that carries the lower tones for bands and orchestras. It is a large wind instrument and as you can imagine it takes a lot of air to create melodious tones. One of the things I loved about playing the Tuba is I loved when the music score called for loud lower instruments, which takes a lot more air. In order to do this, I needed a lot of air in a very short amount of time, especially if the music was moving at a fast tempo.

It is this experience that taught me how efficiently breathe. This tactic is transferable to the skill of speaking in front of an audience.

You have tried the previous breathing exercises, now I want you to try something new. Instead of taking a deep breath only through your nose or your mouth. I want you to take a moment to take a deep breath, but this time, breathe in through your mouth AND your nose at the same time.

This can feel very weird, but if you did it right, you should feel a cold spot in the back of your throat. Did you feel the cold spot? Did you feel a difference in how quickly your lungs filled up?

Efficient breathing techniques is likely a physiologically new to you. Due to this, it will take practice to create this as a habit. I would not recommend trying this for the first time in front of an audience. Until you get a little more comfortable with the technique, it could give your audience the impression that you are gasping for air.

Recommendations for practice:

1. Start while you are at your computer (e.g. responding to emails).
2. Incorporate it in one-on-one conversations (e.g. friends or colleagues)
3. Try it during meetings
4. Implement into your sessions

This slow progression can afford you the opportunity to become accustomed with the technique and eventually will become a habit. Then if your breath is efficient and effective, you're setting the foundation for a confident tone.

Confident tone

To get people to buy into you as a facilitator or presenter, they want to have confidence in you and your tone is a key indicator for them. Think about a learning event you attended, and the speaker did not have a confident tone. What were some of the characteristics you observed?

Possibly the person was soft spoken. Possibly had a tremor in their voice. Possibly seemed disingenuous. Possibly made statements sound like questions.

The ability to convey confidence in your tone starts with your posture. As odd as that may sound, it is valuable. If you are standing straight, shoulders slightly rolled back (not getting too "puffy-chesty"), and your chin slightly above parallel this begins to change your state of mind to a confident one. If your mind is confident, your tone will follow.

It is easy to see if someone that is delivering a session is hunched over (shoulders rolled forward) and chin down, it is likely that the tone being conveyed is timid and soft spoken. This will not enhance credibility nor inspire confidence.

Effective and efficient breathing is a great way to help keep you relaxed. It is when breaths get shorter that I have seen too many good facilitators or presenters begin to get nervous and the tremor starts to show up in their voice. If you are unfamiliar with the voice tremors, it is when you hear a shakiness in someone's voice. You may see this when someone is overly scared or cold.

If you are standing confidently and you have control over your breath, then your voice should be natural and pleasant. Utilizing your natural speaking voice is always a great place to start. It demonstrates your personality, and you remain true to who you are.

Finishing sentences appropriately is the concept of the voice inflection that ends each of your sentences. This may sound like it is a no-brainer however, I have seen individuals come through my classes that struggle with this.

Based on the sentence structure and what sentence you are speaking indicates how you should verbalize the end of each sentence. At the end of a statement, you should end with a slight downward inflection. At the end of a question, you should end with a slight uptick in your inflection. These are indicators to your audience if you are making a point or asking a question you want them to reflect on or answer.

Read the following sentence aloud as it's written:

"Go to the store?"

The structure is intended to be a directive go to the store, however, with the inflection at the end, it sounds more like question. The slight uptick at the end of any statement can confuse an audience and damage your credibility.

This is equivalent to my nieces when they were in their early teen years and it was commonplace for them to end their statements as if there was an understood, "Right?" I found myself asking, "I don't know you tell me." Your audience could be in a similar situation.

Articulation

Articulation is your friend. Being deliberate with your articulations will aid in fostering a confident tone. This means the accurate articulation of words:

"T" sounds are crisp.

- To achieve this, it is ensuring the tip of your tongue flicks on the roof of your mouth.

Vowel sounds are not muttled

- This one can be difficult depending on the country or region you grew up in. Accents and local dialects can cause certain vowel sounds to blend together.
- For instance, there is a different between "alright" and "ah-ight."

"-ing" endings are annunciated.

- Even a slight "guh" or "eeng" where appropriate can assist in the ability to be understood in a larger room.

"K" sounds are clear

- This can be any variation of spelling that calls for clear "K" sound
- "Calls" and "Clear" are good examples.

Keep in mind, that articulation is valuable, the prior tips are not intended to change how you speak (e.g. accents or drawls), but it is something in which every facilitator and presenter should be aware.

The crispness in which we articulate carries through the size of any venue, even if your voice is amplified (e.g. microphone and sound system). It will help ensure you message is understood, and your message is not lost.

These first two elements of your voice are base level concepts, yet they have a symbiotic relationship. Since your confident tone will follow how you stand and present yourself, which we will cover in more detail in the Confidence section. If your posture is timid, withdrawn, or small, your vocal tone will follow. This will show up by not filling the room with your voice, blurry articulation, and mumbling. All of which can disengage an audience.

Dynamic

Voice dynamics is what can capture an audience and keep them focused on your words. They are essentially the "jazz hands" of your voice. You can draw in an audience and bring them to tears. You can also send a bolt of lightning through the soul of an audience that energizes them to conquer the world. It is the ability to use your full range of voice dynamics.

AUTHENTICITY

How you deliver a message to your audience is more important the actual word choice. I have had folks challenge me on this concept. It is accurate to say word choice makes a difference, however the mechanism in which it is delivered is what makes it special.

After spending almost my entire career in the corporate training profession, I believe that Instructional Designers can create the most beautiful content (e.g. verbiage) and it is the job of the facilitator or presenter to breathe life into the content. You can have the most beautifully crafted content or speech drafted, but if it is delivered in a monotone manner, then the audience experience and impact will fall short. The life of the content starts with the facilitators voice.

There needs to be a variation in your voice. The first part of voice variation is drawing your pitch up and down. This is the utilization of the full range of pitch. The higher pitch can drive excitement. The lower pitch can soften a message (e.g. emotional stories). Keep in mind, while delivering to an audience, don't go crazy by trying to make your voice something it's not.

For instance, while facilitating a presentation skills class, a guy in class had a very comfortable tone to his voice when speaking to other and participating is discussions. However, when he got in front of the group, he tried to recreate every late 90s FM radio DJ voice who's counting down the hits. It wasn't authentic and it became quite obnoxious. He wasn't being authentic. When I asked him why his voice changed once he got in front of the group, he had no idea he was over acting. This ultimately took away from his presentation.

The goal of utilizing various pitch ranges is to allow you to demonstrate your personality, which we know authenticity is important to audiences.

The rate of your speech cadence also plays a factor in your voice dynamics, both fast and slow. A slower rate of speech is usually reserved for more emotional connections. It can also help people focus. This slower rate can be powerful when you want to let a message sink in and resonate with an audience. It can also help audience members lean forward in their seats and become even more interested.

You can pair a slower rate of speech with a softer tone to really make an impact. When I was working for a satellite tv company, I was delivering a presentation that was focused on ladder safety. Part of the presentation was focused on the importance of safe ladder operation. To make my point, I shared a story about a technician that was severely injured on a ladder and the impacts it had not only on the technician, but to his family as well. While delivering this portion of the presentation, I intentionally slowed my rate of speech and softened my tone because I wanted to the audience to make the personal connection that it could happen to them. I remember seeing members of the audience lean forward in their seats because it was hitting home for them.

If you are child of the 80s and watched Saturday morning cartoons, you may be familiar with the popular Micro Machines commercial. This commercial for the toy Micro Machines had a guy in the commercial that was the fastest talker I had ever seen. It was part of the advertisement to get kids excited about the "micro machines that miraculously move." Guess what, pretty much every kid in my elementary school had Micro Machines. It got kids excited because the energy was driven by this guy who likely fit three times the number of words in a 30-second commercial than most commercials at that time.

This is the power of utilizing a faster rate of speech during a training or presentation. It can be used to drive excitement, make a fast-moving point, or just have fun.

Word of caution, although it can be fun to incorporate a faster rate of speech, but it is difficult to sustain over time, for not only you but your audience. If you become talented in speaking faster, you need to keep in mind your audience may not have "trained" ears to listen at 2-3 times speed over an extended period of time. In addition, your ability to successfully speak at a faster rate for an extended period of time as a presenter/facilitator is taxing. Your heart rate will inevitably increase, your breathing becomes shallower, and eventually your brain and mouth become out of alignment.

This has happened to me. There has been a number of times when I've increased my rate of speech because I got passionate about a topic and I kept riding that verbal express train and before I knew it, the conductor in my brain pulled the emergency break. While in front of a class, I found myself having an internal dialogue:

"Oh crap, what did I just say?"

"No idea. We were talking about nervous habits."

"Did we hit all of our key points?"

"Uhhh..."

"That's what I thought."

"Quick, ask a question. See what they recall."

As odd as it sounds, I've had those internal conversations in my brain. I would also imagine that the audience could see an odd look on my face as I conducted this internal audit over a 3-5 second time frame.

Utilize the faster rate of speech to spark excitement with your audience, just be careful not to put yourself into a position where your brain and mouth are out of alignment (more on that later).

As we think about the vocal ranges (high/low pitch and slow/fast rate of speech), let's try something to help you find your authentic range.

Read the below passage aloud in your normal speaking voice:

The tickled tortoise teased the timely turkey, while the boxy barracuda bought bagels beside the balmy beach.

Now, read the passage in a falsetto (high pitch) register.

Try it now in the lowest register of your vocal range.

What did you feel?

You likely noticed that when you read it aloud in your high pitch register, you may have felt you spoke a little faster. Then when you read it in your lowest register, your rate of speech was slower. This occurs because your airway becomes smaller when you speak higher which makes it easier to articulate at a faster rate. The inverse is true when you are speaking in a lower register, your airway is open more and it takes a lot more work, so you slow down.

Keep in mind, you will likely not be in a position where you are speaking in those extreme ranges of your vocal capabilities when you're in front of an audience, but you now know your range.

Projection

The concept of projection is to ensure everyone in your audience can hear you. A common misconception is to increase your volume. The downside is this easily translates to shouting. Yes, there is a difference between shouting and projecting.

If you have every been to a dance club where the music is very loud and in order to try and talk to someone, you have to shout. By the end of the night, your throat is dry and likely hurts from having to shout to your friends. The same thing applies when you are in front of an audience. If you are shouting, your voice will be worn out by the end of your session.

Shouting is very directionally focused, in one particular direction. Projection is the idea of filling the entire room with your voice.

If you are unsure if you are doing one or the other, if you are shouting your vocal cords tighten up and if done over an extended period of time, it will cause tension in your neck and shoulders. Shouting drives tension.

On the opposite end, projection is an opening of the vocal cords, which keeps your neck and shoulders relaxed.

The "fuel source" when you are talking is air. When you are in a shouting state, your breaths will be shallower, and you will feel your chest and shoulder raise up when you breathe. This can drive tension in your neck and shoulders as well. If you are efficiently breathing, your breath will go into your belly. You will feel your gut expand. This gives you more air to fill the room while keeping your upper body relaxed.

Here are some tips to help you optimize for projection:

Keep your jaw relaxed.

- If you feel your gritting your teeth and your jaw muscles are tense, you are stressed and likely are shouting.

Open your airways.

- Similar to the efficient breathing technique discussed earlier, this helps open your airways.

- Think about when you are about to yawn, your jaw feels like it is beginning to open and your airways expand to take in as much air as possible.

Control your breath.

- Utilizing the efficient breathing technique will ensure you are filling your "fuel tank" (e.g. lungs) while keeping your airway, neck, and shoulder relaxed.

To practice your projection, use an exercise I learned from American Idol. In 2007, the fifth season of American Idol, Chris Daughtry progressed deep into the competition and during one of the weeks, he had an opportunity to rehearse with Andrea Bocelli (highly acclaimed opera singer). During this session, Andrea had Chris lay on the ground and practice the song he was preparing for his feature that week. That particular exercise helped Chris focus on breathing into his belly while filling up the room.

I have found this exact exercise works well in the training and presentation profession. Next time you are in a larger room, and you want to practice your breathing while filling the room with your voice. Lay down on your back in a corner of the room. Have a colleague, or more if you'd like, lay down on their back in a far point of the room. Once everyone is in position, have a conversation.

This exercise will force you to practice filling the room with your voice while breathing correctly. To help make sure you are filling up your gut and efficiently breathing during this exercise, fold. Your hands comfortably across your belly so you can feel it fill up with air as you interact. Also be mindful of the cold spot in the back of your throat as that is the indicator of practicing your efficient breathing.

When training a training certification class, I had the entire class practice this. They all looked at me funny when I asked everyone to lay on the ground then say someone's name and interact with them. The entire class of 15 then took turns practicing their breathing and filling the room with their voices.

Word Choice

In many cases, as a facilitator, your content is already developed, and you're asked to follow the guide. As a presenter, you may have a prepared speech. It is imperative to understand your audience, there are key words/phrases that may be taboo or that will positively stand out to your audience. Pick up on those key words/phrases and find ways to integrate them into your delivery. This can help build a connection.

The key words can be important because you want your audience to feel like you get them. One area where this is crucial if you are delivering a presentation to an executive or a team of decision makers. There have been many times when I was preparing to meet with an executive and I would do reconnaissance on the individual. I would watch videos they created, if any existed, or I would talk to others that have worked with that individual to know what is on the priority list for them.

One particular time, when I started at a prominent financial services firm, one of the main customers of my learning team was a Senior Vice President for the contact center. I talked to at least seven different people to better understand who he was and what was on his "wish list" for the training team supporting his organization. I remember "impact" and "synergies" were the two common themes that surfaced. You better believe I intentionally incorporated examples to those two areas, while using those words.

Keep in mind, I wasn't giving a formal presentation, but the concept is exactly the same. Even if your audience is one person, it is vital to establish credibility by getting the person to connect with what you're saying. You want the audience to feel that you understand them and/or what *THEY* need to succeed.

Another common area of word choice that I've debated with others throughout my career is swearing. I have worked with many individuals that say that a presenter or facilitator should never swear when in front of an audience.

When I get asked, "Can I swear?" my response is always:

FUCK YES!

I've been criticized for utilizing swear words. I hold the belief that they are just words. Just know, it *MUST* fit into your vernacular and your authentic style. It can drive impact and catch attention. It is also imperative you know your audience.

If delivering a speech at a church, I'd recommend censoring yourself, as it could be a great way to turn people's ears off. Having an incorrect word or phrase can immediately disconnect and audience. If they are turned off by colorful language then that audience member will spend more time thinking about the word you chose and not pay attention to your message or content.

Regardless of the roles I've held throughout my career, I have always been open to inviting others to observe on of my sessions. I look at as an opportunity to receive feedback from anyone so it can help me gain new perspectives and if it works out, perhaps that individual can glean some ideas of how I approach a session. In one particular instance, I was training a class in Dallas, and I'd invited a tenured member of my team to observe the session I was delivering. During the session, I referenced the sign I had in my office, and still do to this day. The sign reads, "Do Cool Shit." This came up off script from the facilitator guide as we were discussing innovation.

Afterwards, we were debriefing the session and the team member of mine told me, "I really don't think you should be cursing when training a class."

We had a healthy discussion about why I incorporated it. I mentioned I wasn't trying to be cool; I referenced the sign as a concept on how to think about innovation and in that particular instance, I could tell there was a bit of a lull in energy. That targeted word choice at the moment caught the attention of the group. It drove some chuckles from the group, and it immediately drove more engagement from the group. Needless to say, there is a time and place.

If it fits your style and it can have a positive effect on your audience, fucking swear. Don't be that awkward person that throws in "Shit" into their class or speech and it feels like Bambi trying to walk for the first time.

Gestures

There are two areas of your body that are your primary gesture machines: hands and face. Both of which build trust and value to messages.

When you are talking to someone, we look at them. Not only for connection and ensure we are focused on what is being said, but it is also for interpretation. Albert Mehrabian was a professor at UCLA and his study became a foundation to better understand how we interpret messages and it is not just through the words that exit our face. His study identified that 7% of the interpretation of our message comes through the words we speak. Then 38% of the message is interpreted through our voice, while 55% of our message comes through body messaging (e.g. gestures).

This study is the bedrock on how we are show up as presenters and facilitators. If we are unable to exemplify what we are speaking to through our gestures, our audience could doubt what we are attempting to convey.

Think about this, if you are talking to someone and they say something to the effect of "This idea is so amazing and I can barely control my excitement," yet their hands are in their pockets and there is zero expression on their face (e.g. stone faced). Would you walk away from that conversation with a high level of excitement? I feel very confident that your response would be a big fat NO.

Your facial expressions are a powerful tool. You need to use it to your advantage.

The best facial gesture that can create a beautiful connection with your audience is your smile. I have found that a true, genuine smile can draw an audience in. When I mention a genuine smile, that means smiling into your eyes. We have seen folks in our lives that can give a fake smile and we know it. When the orbicularis oculi muscles, which are the primary muscles that surround your eyes, are activated in a smile that is when the smile goes into the eyes.

AUTHENTICITY

Fake Smile (Not smiling into the eyes)

Genuine Smile (Smiling into the eyes)

Keep in mind, the smile is a weapon and keeping it prevalent is important. However, it is in your best interest to not maintain a creepy smile throughout your session. When it is there all the time, even when the messaging may be somber, you will begin to look like Batman's nemesis, The Joker. Then things get awkward.

The other big component for gestures is your hands. As weird as it sounds, but utilizing your hands and keeping them visible subconsciously builds trust.

Imagine for a moment, you are walking down the street and someone walks up to with their hands behind their back and they say, "EXCUSE ME!"

AUTHENTICITY

What is your first gut response? Likely you hesitate. Perhaps even begin to worry because you're wondering, what they need and more importantly, wondering what they are holding behind their back. This reaction is triggering your "fight or flight" response.

Although extreme, the concept remains. If the audience is unable to see your hands consistently, this can create a very subtle disconnect with your audience.

Utilize gestures to compliment your point. This can be fairly easy because it is innate in all of to incorporate our hands when we are speaking. It accents our points and adds a visual element to words.

It is something that we learn as kids. Think about the song, "The Itsy-Bitsy Spider." If you learned this song as a kid (you are likely humming the song right now, you're welcome for the ear worm), you want to start moving your hands to match the song. This is the common practice of taking your thumbs and placing them against the opposing hands index finger then as you sing the song, you take bottom two finger pairs and shift them to the top. The intent is to add a visual element for kids to replicate a spider climbing up a waterspout.

The same applies when we are in front of an audience. We want to ensure it matches the words we are saying.

Try this, if you think of the word "holistic," what hand gesture would you use to capture the essence of that word? For me, my first instinct is to take both of my hands and create a motion that would indicate a spherical type of image almost as if I am running my hands around the outside of a ball. Your visual concept of the word may be different and that's ok. There is not one gesture for each word. That is the beauty of each person's style, there will be variations that match each style. It is not like the *Lord of the Rings* where there is *one gesture to rule them all*.

There are two common questions I have received when it comes to gestures:

1. What do I do if I've been told not to use my hands when I'm presenting/facilitating?
2. How can I use my hands if I am holding something like a marker or note pages?

Both are legit questions.

In the event someone coaches you and tells you not to use your hands, I would recommend doing a quick audit of your hands.

Your quick gesture audit should be to answer these two questions:

1. Are my gestures distracting from my message?
2. Are my gestures mismatched from my message?

If you can answer "no" to both of those questions, here is what I would recommend:

- Accept the feedback
- Thank them
- Keep being yourself

Feedback is gold. You always want to accept it especially because the person observing you took the time to observe and capture notes for you. Yet, I have learned it is more important utilize the feedback that helps you become better but doesn't take you away from your authentic delivery style.

The craziest instance I've witnessed is I was working with a lady from New

AUTHENTICITY

York and we were having a virtual meeting and something seemed off with her. She didn't seem herself. This particular colleague was high energy and always very animated, it is what made her a good facilitator, however on this particular day her energy was down and was not animated at all. I eventually had to ask her if she was ok. She mentioned that she recently received feedback from another colleague of ours that she shouldn't talk with her hands. So, during our meeting, she was literally sitting on her hands to avoid speaking with her hands. This was the only way she could control her natural urge to gesture when facilitating or in this case, meeting virtually. I felt awkward for her.

I ended up telling her that although I appreciate where the feedback was coming from, it was taking away from what made her special as a facilitator. By limiting her natural energy which was expressed through her hand movements, it took away from her authenticity.

The moral of the story: Don't sit on your hands.

As to the second question, how can I use my hands if I am holding something like a marker or note pages?

The short answer is to treat it like an extension of your appendage.

Instead of thinking of restricting yourself by holding something or feeling as if you can't use your hands because you are holding something, gesture as if it is part of your hand.

When you're holding notes, you can absolutely keep them in your hand and reference them, and if you're stepping to the side of the screen to point out something on the screen, motion with your hand that contain the notes.

Many times, in training classes, we are utilizing a dry eraser board and have a marker in our hand. The same thing applies, however there is a subtle ninja trick that can help.

Gesture while palming the marker.

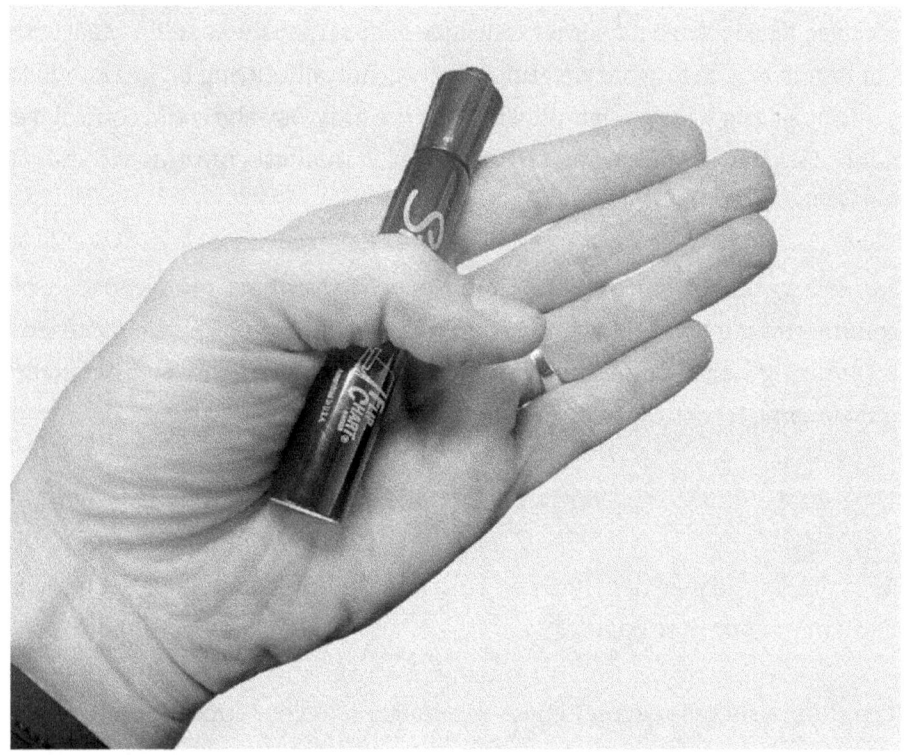

By tucking the marker in the groove of your hand between your thumb and index finger as seen in the image above, you are now able to freely gesture.

The marker can also act like a pointer. If you are documenting process steps on easel paper or a dry erase board, you can utilize the marker to point to specific steps that have been covered already.

One of the best examples I've ever seen is Simon Sinek's Puget Sound TEDx Talk from September 2009, which as of the writing of this book has over

63 million views. During this video where Simon highlights his concept of Start with Why, he does a masterful job of delivering his talk using easel paper and one marker. When you watch this video, you will notice how seamlessly Simon never draws attention to his marker and points to the various circles he's drawn with his palmed marker. To add to the complexity of his presentation, he not only is balancing between drawing on the paper and gesturing with the maker, but he is also smoothly juggling a microphone. It is a masterful demonstration of how to capture attention while not drawing attention to the fact his hands are full. Needless to say, he never showed his duck butt.

Eye Contact

When I've delivered sessions on training and presentation skills, I will ask my audience, how long should you hold eye contact?

The answers are pretty consistent. Responses are usually between 2-10 seconds. The approximate baseline is around 3-5 seconds. The intent is to engage each person in the room. You want them to feel seen.

In one particular class, I asked the above question and one person actually responded with a confident 30 seconds. Think about that. If you are an audience member and the presenter or facilitator looked at you for 30 seconds, it would start to get creepy. You better believe I had some fun with this individual.

When this learner mentioned 30 seconds, I responded, "Ok, let's think about this for a moment. If I were to stare at you for 30 seconds during a session, there would come a moment when you may start to feel uncomfortable because you may start wondering why is this person staring at just me. Did I do something wrong? Do I have something on my face? When is this guy going to stop staring at me."

While I am saying this, I am moving a little closer and never breaking eye contact. It was quite interesting to watch the reaction because this particular learner visibly started to become uncomfortable. He broke his eye contact with me and began shifting nervously in his chair.

Once I saw his comfort level was impacted, I posed a new question, "Do you think 30 seconds may be a little too long?" He got the point.

The other part of eye contact comes with actively listening to the audience members.

If you are facilitating there will be times throughout your session where learners will ask questions or want to provide insight into the subject matter. When you are presenting, there may be less "give and take" since it is one-way communication, yet depending on the event there may be Q&A or when you WOW an audience, folks will want to talk to you after the fact. Both instances are ideal to lean into your active listening.

This is something I had to really work at throughout my career. Early on, when listening to an audience member I had a tendency to remain "stone faced" (e.g. no expression) which for me came across as RBF (Resting Bitch Face). Even if it was an interesting question or point being made, nothing would show on my face. This is not an experience you want to create for your audience.

The first thing you want to ensure you're doing is maintain eye contact. This immediately demonstrates a level of interest in the audience member and what they are saying. This helps to ensure you are locked in and focused. More importantly, you are giving the audience member the impression that the point they are making is the most important thing in your world at that moment.

If it is an interesting point, raise your eyebrows. This provides a subtle signal to the audience member that you feel the point is interesting. You may even throw in a slight head tilt to the side, which has been known to be a non-verbal cue that you are intrigued by the question, or the point being made.

If it is a humorous point being made, smile and even chuckle. You want the audience member to feel heard and appreciated for the humor they are bringing. This can be valuable because it opens the door for others to inject humor into the session, so you are not the one that is always keeping things lighthearted.

If a question is being asked, flash an inquisitive look on your face. This could be a simple lip pursing with a widening of the eyes. It is important to remain focused on questions so you are able to deploy the question processing flow, which we will cover later.

The subtle nuances associated to non-verbal cues can be quite powerful and if you really want to nerd out on these, I highly recommend Vanessa Van Edwards book Cues. She dives deep into all the nuances associated with non-verbals, which has helped me tremendously in my ability to engage audience members during my sessions.

Keep in mind, every presenter and facilitator will be different. How you emote on your face will be different than how I show emotion. That is ok.

Due to this difference, I encourage you to think about the face you would make in the different circumstances. Let's try it.

What face would you make if someone told you something intriguing and you want to learn more? Make that face now.

What face would you make if someone told a humorous story? Make that face now.

What face would you make if someone is asking you a question during a session? Make that face now.

Sustaining eye contact and actively listening to audience members enhances your credibility as you demonstrate an investment into what he or she are stating or asking.

Your ability to remain authentic with your audience is paramount to keep your audience engaged. Authenticity centers around the key elements:

- Movement
- Voice
- Word Choice
- Gestures
- Eye Contact

By understanding these elements and putting them into practice will position you to remain credible with your audience and prevent your audience "BS Alarms" from going off.

6

CONFIDENCE

Presence

Not to be confused with one's physical self being in a particular location, Presence is how you carry yourself. Presence is the passion you bring to the situation. Presence is remaining in the moment. Presence IS the WOW-Factor!

Being able to demonstrate a strong presence in front of an audience is a fascinating. Some individuals have a natural proclivity to demonstrate a strong presence, where others need to invest a lot of intentional effort to develop the skill. It is also the skill-set that can easily over-rotate into a perceived arrogance. Presence is a demonstration of confidence that focuses on enhancing the lives of others.

Confidence vs Arrogance

There is the difference between confident and arrogant. According to the New Oxford American Dictionary, here is how each are defined:

- Arrogant (adj.) - having or revealing an exaggerated sense of one's own importance or abilities.
- Confident (adj.) - feeling or showing confidence in oneself; self-assured.

As presenters and trainers, we flirt with that line often. It is important to have confidence in your abilities and the deliver the experience that is required. Arrogance begins to creep into our psyche when we begin thinking we are infallible. This can start to show up after we've had a string of successful sessions or immense amount of people telling how much they enjoy you and your sessions. Let's be honest, that feels amazing. Everyone loves to hear the positive feedback.

With the skill-set of capturing an audience, it is important to maintain a level of humility. The humility comes with knowing we can be better. For me, I have been caught in that trap before. When I was training a lot of trainer certification classes, I found a rhythm for the experience I wanted to create and it was met with positive receptions by my audiences. This bled into other classes I would facilitate. I began thinking I didn't need to prepare as much or could just show up and deliver a similar experience. I was humbled quickly when I received feedback that wasn't up to the standard I'd grown accustomed to receiving. It was constructive insights offered by the learners, but it was the lesson I needed.

Humility is the anchor that keeps us from becoming arrogant.

Needless to say, regression into arrogance can occur. It is a fine line between arrogance and confidence. If you want to be great, you need to dance with the line while being cautious to not step across into the arrogance realm. Your audience will know, and they won't be shy telling you, either to your face or in post-session feedback.

If you want to display a strong presence for your audiences, below are some ideas to help you maintain a high level of presence that displays confidence and avoids arrogance.

- **Observe others.**
  Take the opportunity to observe other great speakers, especially in person. This can push you realize there is room for improvement. This can even mean observing someone you work with that you feel is great in front of an audience and watch how they create an exceptional experience, then add it to your toolbox.

- **Remain in the moment.**
  If you have things going on outside of your session (e.g. sick loved one), there is nothing you can do about it while you are in your session. Park those outside the room and when your session is complete, you can pick them up. You owe it to your audience to remain focused on them and their experience.

- **Demonstrate passion.**
  Make sure you are passionate about the subject or topic you are delivering to your audience. Yes, there may be times you are asked to deliver a session on something you are not insanely passionate about, but it is your responsibility as a presenter/facilitator to find what about that session you can be passionate about. This may mean additional preparation on your part to talk to others and learn from them.

Your presence is one of the first things your audience will judge you on. The additional items within this confidence section will also help enhance your presence.

Being "On"

Something interesting I stumbled across throughout my career journey, some of the best facilitators/presenters are natural introverts. Being a natural introvert, I am not the type of person that needs interaction with others to fuel me. Most introverts don't. After sessions I've delivered, I have had attendees ask me, "where does your energy come from?" I've also been asked, "how are you such an extrovert?" Don't get me wrong, when I get in front of an audience, I consume the energy from the group like a sow bellying up to the trough at feeding time. I gobble it up.

I along with my fellow introverts have the ability to "flip the switch." The switch being the ability to get into the mode for being in front of an audience. When I flip my switch, it is go-time. I am fully committed. My energy is up, my focus is lasered in, and my introverted self gets put on the bench.

The concept of "Being On" is centered around the mindset shift. Finding a strong Preparation sequence (covered during Preparation), can help to get you to the point of Being On. My internal dialogue before a session has included the phrase, "It's Showtime." Yes, it's corny, but it works for me. When I've leveraged this along with my Preparation Sequence, that is when I know it was time to be on.

Being "on" can be equated to flipping a light switch to the "on" position. What happens when you flip a light switch to the "on" position? The light comes on. Things get brighter.

The flipping of the switch became prevalent for me because as a natural introvert, I needed a mental toggle that could get me out of my natural state.

Something interesting to think about, there is a high likelihood that most that will read this book are natural introverts. During a span when I was leading a team full of talented facilitators, over 60% of the team of 26 facilitators were natural introverts. You would have no idea they were quiet by nature because they could flip the switch and focus on the audience experience.

Every person will get themselves ready to be "On" in their own way. I worked with gifted facilitator and his process was that once the room is set up, he would disappear. I finally had to ask him, "where did you go?" He told me he needed to find a quiet place, usually a separate unoccupied room, and he would do full body movements (e.g. touching his toes, jumping up/down) and he would talk to himself out loud to get himself ready.

For those that may be extroverted, your switch may be a little different. Instead of trying to identify how to get your energy up and bench your introvert, you may find you need to dedicate time to switch to audience mode. In my experience, extroverts tend to want to talk about everything during a session, which can derail timing and negatively impact the overall experience. So, extroverts may need to switch that mindset from full conversation mode to presentation mode that focuses on the objective of the session.

Wherever you may land, introvert or extrovert, it is important to know where you may have blind spots, so you know not only how to flip your switch but the purpose of the switch you are flipping.

Charisma

Think about a time when you were drawn to another person, but you couldn't figure out why. You found yourself wanting to be around that person. Who comes to mind for you? The person you are envisioning likely has charisma.

Charisma is a term that is utilized to describe another person that has "it."

"It" being the personality traits that others are drawn toward like a moth to a flame. It is true, some may have more of a natural proclivity, but it is completely possible to develop the skill.

Charisma can be demonstrated by:

- Expressing genuine interest in others
- Telling stories others enjoy or can relate to
- Making eye contact
- Smiling

Expressing genuine interest

This is a quality when you actually care about another person. This comes through active listening and inquiring more about the other person. Both elements demonstrate to someone that you are engaged in the moment WITH them. Like the active listening mentioned earlier, the other person should feel heard. When it comes to inquiries these should be casual in nature. When expressing interest in someone else, it should feel like a conversation, not an interrogation.

Telling stories other enjoy or can relate to

Telling stories can be very relatable to others, especially if it is applicable to the circumstance. Throughout the years, I have experienced thousands of story situations during the sessions I've delivered, most of which only surface in the moment. This situation occurs for me when in a session, an attendee may ask a question about how to handle a particular situation, this then sparks the story recall that I can leverage to help address the question. You will find that your ability to recall stories becomes easier over time with more experience.

There are times when scripting a story for your session is needed because it can be valuable for your audience. These types of stories can be pulled from your experience, which is preferable, or in certain situations you are able to tell a compelling story that occurred to someone else.

I have utilized the story from a former colleague of mine and good friend. We were co-facilitating a presentation session together and she told the story about how others had interpreted credibility of a presenter by the shine on their shoes. In this particular example, the presenter delivered a quality presentation and upon leaving, the room of leaders noticed the scuff marks all over the presenter's shoes that looked like he grabbed his shoes out of a meat grinder.

The group spent more time talking about the shoes than the content of the presentation. The point she made was how you show up, especially the care on appearance, can demonstrate confidence and enhance credibility with audiences. Needless to say, I have incorporated that story as it is a great example, even though it wasn't one I directly observed.

Within certain settings, it can be valuable to leverage a story from others, HOWEVER you want to use them sparingly as it could work against your credibility.

Storytelling Tips

Use similes and metaphors:

- **Simile** - a figure of speech comparing two unlike things that is often introduced by like or as
- **Metaphor** - a figure of speech in which a word or phrase literally denoting one kind of object or idea is used in place of another to suggest a likeness or analogy between them

Utilizing similes and metaphors create a visual picture for the listeners.

It is important to ensure it is relatable to the situation.

- If you're asked, "why is the sky blue?" Don't respond to the question with a story about the first time you ran a mile.

Don't ramble.

- If your story gets too long, the minds of the audience members will begin to wander, especially wondering where you are going with the story.

Make use of humor.

- More in the next section. In short, if people enjoy the story and it can make them giggle, they will enjoy it and they will remain engaged in the story.

Making eye contact and smiling.

- Both of these concepts were covered in Authenticity, and they help drive your charisma, both on and off the stage

Humor

"How can I be funny? I'm not a naturally funny person."

This is a common response I have received throughout the years when working with trainers and presenters. In many instances, the individuals mentioning this are not giving themselves enough credit. At some point in time, in all our lives, we have made others laugh. Perhaps it was being silly, telling a joke, conveying a humorous story, or doing something outlandish. We have all made someone smile or laugh in our life.

Humans love to smile and laugh; it is good for the soul.

For me, I grew up watching sitcoms and movies. This has helped me gain a perspective on various elements that have a humorous effect on others. I watched so many movies, I have even been "complimented" on my ability to recall movie lines and quotes. So much so, a former co-worker of mine bought me a shirt that reads, "I speak fluent movie quotes." Although it is not a compliment most would hold in high regard, it is definitely one of my favorites.

This exposure to funny movies and sitcoms has helped me to incorporate variations of humor into my sessions. It doesn't mean I always quote movies, but if the moment is right, I can utilize an apt movie quote or reference. I have found that referencing movies is a staple that most can relate to. Pretty much everyone has seen a movie or two in their life.

Keep in mind, knowing your audience is important. There was an instance when I overly anticipated the relatability of a movie reference with a particular audience. I was training a class in Grand Junction, CO and I was talking about voice dynamics. So as some may anticipate, I referenced Ben Stein, the teacher from *Ferris Buellers Day Off* (popular movie in the 80s starring Matthew Broderick).

In this particular scene, Ben Stein was taking attendance, and he was using a very monotone voice and when the camera showed the students they were all day-dreaming or sleeping.

Unfortunately, reality slapped me in the face when I received blank stares. Come to find out, not a single person in the class was born prior to 1990 and no one in the class ever heard of the movie (Oops). Definitely not one of my shining moments.

I don't mention this as a recommendation to start watching every movie ever made, but it is to reinforce the concept to use what works for you and what may resonate with your audience.

Another simple, yet highly effective, use of humor is of the self-deprecating variety. As our audience sizes increase, the scope of experience and personalities grows, what is funny to you won't always be funny or relatable to everyone in your audience. This is where self-deprecating humor comes into place.

This is the type of humor that you poke fun of yourself.

Here are some examples of how I've used self-deprecating humor:

1. When I have worked with groups, and we are discussing appearance. I have talked about having your hair styled and not looking you just rolled out of bed. Being a bald person, when I get to that moment, I mention this is important for most, and not for those "follicly-challenged" like myself.

2. When I have contracted to deliver content for a prominent training organization, one of the selling points in the course introduction mentions the classes are "Facilitated by Experts." I mention to the class that with me leading the class that they are playing rather fast and loose with the term "expert."

- Side note, this may seem like I am diminishing my credibility, they have already been exposed to the experience I bring to the session (20 years facilitating and over 10,000 hours delivering sessions), so it adds levity to the situation. It also is a way to incorporate humor early into the session to let the audience know I want them to enjoy their journey.

Although these are examples of what has worked for me, it is important to find your style. There have been numerous facilitators/presenters I have observed that were humorous and I was awestruck of their ability to engage their audience with humor. However, what works for them may not work for me. An example is I was speaking at the Udemy Innovation Summit in 2018, one of my fellow speakers, Francesca Gino told a humorous story that related to her being a mom and her Italian heritage. It was amazing, but neither of which I could demonstrate, as I am not a mom nor Italian.

One word of caution as you begin to dance in the humor space, try to avoid humor associated to audience members, politics, or religion. Those can be very sensitive subjects and could easily offend audience members.

Being Present

Life happens to all of us. Whether it is an argument with your significant other, car gets a flat tire, water heater breaks, kid gets suspended from school, life events happen that can throw us off our game. What makes these types of situations difficult is they hi-jack our thought process and will usually become the number one priority at that moment.

You are reading this book because you feel drawn to be great in front of an audience and life situations can derail you from creating that experience for your audience.

In order to maintain focus on your audience, it starts with a mindset shift. It starts with visualizing a little red wagon.

Take a moment think about a little red wagon. It could be one you had as a kid or one you've seen in a picture. The one I picture is the old school metal red wagon that has the long black metal handle that pulls the wagon. There are black wheels with white rims. At the center of the white rim is a little red cap that covers the bolts that hold the wheels onto the frame. On the side of the red wagon, the words "Radio Flyer" are emblazoned in white.

The little red wagon you're envisioning may look different than mine and that's ok. The point is I want you to think of a wagon in detail.

This little red wagon is what we pull around with us every single day. Inside this little red wagon are all the things, or baggage, we carry with us every single day. Our successes. Our failures. Our life events. When you think about it, these are the things that take our focus and our brain capacity. Usually, the more urgent things are sitting right on top of the load as they are taking up most of our thoughts.

Now that we've painted this mental image of our wagon and all the "baggage" we carry with us each day, I want you to think of a room in which you've delivered a session. If you have never presented or trained a class before, think of a class you've attended and the room you are in. With the image of that room, put yourself at the front of the room with your audience in their seats. Are you picturing yourself up front about ready to deliver the greatest session ever?

As you are getting ready to dominate this session, picture yourself needing to pull your little red wagon with all your "baggage" around the room.

Feels awkward, doesn't it?

Whether you realize it or not, if you are pulling your metaphorical little red wagon around with you in front of an audience, it will be just as awkward as literally pulling a wagon around a room while delivering a session.

If you are distracted or worried about the contents in your little red wagon, it will impact your ability to deliver an exceptional session and your audience will sense it.

To help ensure you are able to remain present in the moment, the mindset shift you need to take is to park your little red wagon outside the door of the room of your session. This helps you transition into focusing on your audience and not focusing on the "baggage" in your little red wagon. If you think about it, when you are in front of your audience, there is nothing you can do about those life events.

The goal with being present is to ensure your audience feels they are the most important thing in your world at that moment.

Nervous Habits

The dreaded nervous habits. When you are putting in the effort to deliver the best experience, a nervous habit is what can derail your message and distract your audience. Interestingly enough, they wreak havoc on a presenter and facilitators psyche. I have seen individuals almost become paralyzed in thought due to a nervous habit that is occurring during a session or a nervous habit they are putting all their effort into avoiding.

What makes things worse is there is so much worry about being judged or maintaining credibility that facilitators and presenters can get completely thrown off their game if a small nervous habit shows up even once. For instance, I have seen numerous individuals lose their train of thought if they say "uh" or "um" one time while in front of an audience. It is important to keep in mind, what habits are.

A habit as defined by the New Oxford American Dictionary is "a settled or regular tendency or practice, especially one that is hard to give up."

In the case of uttering an "uh/um," it is a filler word that usually surfaces when transitioning from one thought to another or a dead air filler. The issue isn't that it is said, which I have done numerous times throughout my career, it is the frequency that becomes an issue.

Most audience members can become so attuned to nervous habits, they can begin counting the frequency upon which they show up. There was an instance where I observed an audience member during a session that was conducting a teach-back where "uh/um" made an appearance 47 times during a 5-minute presentation.

This equates to 9.4 "uh/um's" every minute. THAT is a nervous habit, and it became a complete distraction.

There are nuances listed in this section that may seem like natural behavior. Where it becomes a problem is when they show up so often that it becomes distracting to your message.

Let's take a look at the most common nervous habits.

Filler words

Filler words are one of the most recognizable nervous habit. They can show up due to a number of different reasons:

- Uncertainty of subject matter
- Attendance of audience member (e.g. upper-level management)
- Being observed, usually for feedback purposes
- Worry of being judged
- First time through content
- Mouth working faster than the brain

This last one is a situation when nerves are riding so high that a person will speak faster to fill the air and the ability to process what is being said is not moving as fast. If you've ever had this happen to you, it is the situation when you catch yourself thinking, "did I actually just say that?" If you've never had that happen, good on you, but it has happened to me countless times.

As many can attest, "uh's" and "um's" are the most common filler words. We've all had these show up when we're speaking. Here's the bad news, they are going to show up. The good news is they are going to show up because they are words. If they do, try not to immediately panic. Just remember, they are words. Even the most seasoned pro has them show up from time to time.

Here's the even crazier part, since this skill-set is ever evolving, you may find yourself moving past "uh/ums," which is great, however filler words can evolve as well.

This evolution shifts from filler words (e.g. filling dead air) to what I call Anchor Words. These are the over usage of specific words that come across as a dependent relationship between you and the word. It can be an evolution from monosyllabic words (e.g. "uh/ums") to multisyllabic words that show up at excessive volumes.

This happened to me.

Early on, I was training a lot of certification classes, and I knew the content backward and forward. I was feeling great. My boss wanted to do an observation to see how the classes were going. Nervousness is not what I was feeling, I was actually excited to him to come in and see the exceptional experience. Then it happened.

I was hitting all the key points, I was modeling the behaviors necessary for learners, and the class was enjoying it. What I didn't know is this sneaky little anchor word showed up. To make matters worse, I didn't even know that sucker showed up until it came time for feedback.

We sat down that night to talk through the day. He was asking the right questions about how I thought the session went, I felt good overall. I knew there were a couple mishaps but nothing out of hand. Until we got to nervous habits on the observation form. He asked me, "was there a word that you possibly overused?"

As I racked my brain, nothing was coming to mind. He told me that "absolutely" showed up thirty-two times. My heart sank. Not because it happened, but because I couldn't recall the over usage (great example of mouth working faster than the brain). He mentioned that it showed up after every time a learner answered a question.

It was certainly a situation when a multisyllabic word became an anchor in my vernacular while I was training.

Twitches

These types of nervous habits happen more of than you may think and the majority of the time they are unconsciously occurring. When individuals get nervous, these twitches tend to be coping mechanisms.

Every person that has a twitch may have their own subtle nuance that surfaces. The two most common twitches I've seen are winking/blinking and massaging.

The winking or blinking begins to occur when someone becomes nervous and one, or both, of their eyes begin opening and closing excessively. Don't get me wrong, we all need to blink, yet when this nervous habit surfaces the volume of the blinking becomes excessive and it no longer appears natural.

The other common one is massaging. Keep in mind, when I have seen this, the facilitators or presenters are not walking through the room massaging the shoulders of the audience members, that would be weird upon itself.

The massaging comes when they begin rubbing a small area of their person. This can show up through the excessive:

- Wringing of the hands
- Stroking a thumb and index finger together
- Caressing one's own forearm
- Rubbing an ear lobe

This last one is one of the most unique I've observed. This particular audience member was an intelligent person, yet fairly soft-spoken. However, when the time came to participate or speak in class, she immediately began rubbing her right ear lobe. I didn't think much of it at first, but when it occurred anytime she spoke, it became evident that this was a coping mechanism for her when she had to speak in front of others.

Constant Pacing

This particular instance is a direct result of individuals that have an immense amount of nervous energy, and it comes out in constant movement across the room. When I've talked to presenters and facilitators that suffer from this, they struggle with remaining still in one spot for a period of time when in front of an audience.

The pacing shows up primarily in two different ways, the "lion in a cage" and the "trainer box step."

Think about a time you went to the zoo, and you stopped by the lion cage. At some point, you've likely seen the lion pacing back and forth along the enclosure. From one side of the cage to the other, then back again. This is the visual that occurs when trainers/presenters are pacing back and forth in a straight line, non-stop.

Now imagine watching an audience watching a trainer/presenter pace back and forth in the front of the room. They will look like they are watching a slow-motion tennis match. Heads moving back and forth.

The other nervous pacing that commonly shows up is the "trainer box step." This is the situation when a presenter/facilitator is moving their feet excessively but not really going anywhere. If you watch his/her feet, they are making a box shape. One step forward, one step to the left, one step back, then one step to the right. This is done over and over again.

Both examples are an example of the nervous energy escaping through their feet. There is so much energy built up, that their body unconsciously moves their feet in a repetitive pattern.

Separation from Audience

Separation is when the presenter/facilitator nervously moves as far away from the audience as possible. This can show up in situations when the subject matter is an unfamiliar topic or one that the presenter/facilitator is not comfortable with. When that occurs, there is a subtle backing away from the audience.

It is almost an unconscious behavior to try and hide from the topic due to lack of confidence.

There have been situations when I have facilitators almost back themselves into the front corner of the room. In one particular instance, if the facilitator was a cartoon, there would've been a hole in the wall in the shape of their body as they quickly exited the room, similar to what is seen in old "Tom &

Jerry" cartoons.

Blocking Oneself Off from the Audience

Similar to creating separation, this can show up due to lack of confidence. Instead of moving away from the audience, facilitators or presenters will find a way to create a barrier between themselves and the audience.

One form of an unconscious barrier is the hands. The hands can create a barrier and the hands clasp together in front of the facilitator for extended period of times.

Another blocker is when the facilitator or presenter places their hand on the side of their neck, possibly begins rubbing the side of the neck. Both of these behaviors are an innate behavior of humans when they are uncomfortable. This usually indicates their "fight or flight" mechanism is overriding their behavior and they are covering vital parts of their body.

Objects are another barrier that are created in uncertain situations. These can truly be anything that creates a disconnect between the person speaking and the audience. It could be a table, podium, mic stand, or easel stand. Each of these objects have a specific purpose and can/should be utilized for the purpose in which they are intended, not for creating separation between the speaker and the audience.

The other common, yet very subtle barrier are the legs. Yes, it may sound odd, but behaviorally it is an indicator of uncertainty or discomfort. This will usually show up when the presenter/facilitator crosses their legs while standing. The overlap usually occurs at the ankle level. This has shown up as a safety mechanism for some.

The most unique example I have ever seen, I was training a presentations skills class with a group of new managers. This lady inadvertently checked all the boxes of each barrier in one fell swoop. At one point of her presentation, she crossed her legs at the ankles, crossed her arms in front of her, while clasping her hands together in front of herself, which occurred after she backed up to the front wall and tucked behind a chair. Barriers upon barriers. When asked, she mentioned that she was very nervous for her short presentation.

Keep in mind, the separation and barriers can be very subtle in nature, but they are great indicators that someone's nerves are working overtime.

Messing with Hair

Although not one that I have to worry about since I'm bald, but it is quite common, especially in female presenters/facilitators.

This is primarily driven by having longer hair, usually shoulder length. That does not preclude those that have short hair from not stumbling into this trap. Even those with short hair have been known to repeatedly draw attention to their hair.

Repetitive messing with hair shows up in variety of different ways. Brushing hair over the ear, twirling the ends of the hair, running hand/fingers through hair, or moving hair away from eyes.

These circumstances can happen naturally because let's face it, sometimes hair does not want to cooperate or the environment can cause situations.

In conversations with female presenters/facilitators, environment for hair plays a factor, namely humidity. From what I've been told, humidity does not help hair for most that have a lot of hair. This is something that should be accounted for, especially when preparing for a session.

Moving in Place

Similar to the nervous habit of constant pacing, this particular common habit is based on movement, however it does not include moving to other locations in the room.

Swaying is the biggest culprit. This is the movement that consists of the presenter/facilitator that shifts back and forth in place. It can be shifting one's weight from one foot to the other or even moving the hips back and forth.

Any time I have seen a presenter/facilitator moving their hips back and forth, I am reminded of the line from the movie "Happy Gilmore" when Happy's golf coach, played by Carl Weathers, is trying to get Happy, played by Adam Sandler, to relax when he is putting. He comes up behind Happy and while reaching around him to grab the putter Happy is holding and begins swaying back and forth uttering the line, "It's all in the hips." Believe me when I tell you, I am not the only one that has thought of that line when that is observed. As a presenter/facilitator, you want your audience to remain focused on your message not thinking of a 90s comedy movie.

Nervous Laughter

In many cases this can be overlooked as it may come across as lightheartedness. Laughing with your audience or even giggling at yourself can be endearing, however when the constant repetition of short bursts of laughs/giggles (e.g. he he) can actually work against credibility.

The nervous laughter is usually observed when punctuating statements, possibly in an attempt to solicit laughter by laughing at your own humor/joke.

In most cases, this nervous laughter shows up when the presenter/facilitator is uncertain or uncomfortable with a topic or may be trying too hard to set a jovial tone with the audience.

I promise you, if you are able to connect with your audience, there will be plenty of times to laugh WITH your audience. It is important to try not to force it by laughing constantly. The last thing you want is for your audience to feel like their session is being led by Batman's archnemesis, The Joker.

Fiddling with Accessories

It is just that, anxious messing with accessories.

Necklaces, especially if longer, are one of the biggest culprits. This usually shows up when a presenter/facilitator loops their finger/thumb just inside the bottom loop of the necklace and moves their hand back and forth. This can easily become a visual distraction for an audience.

Similar to necklaces, badge lanyards are common visual distractions. These become easier to fiddle with because most lanyards hang lower from the neck, sometimes hanging as low as the waistline. Due to the nature of the lanyard hanging so low, it is too tempting to grab the badge and move it back and forth.

There have been instances when I've seen presenters/facilitators fiddle with their badge when it is attached to their belt via a retractable lanyard.

During an observation, I witnessed a trainer continue to extend his badge from his belt line and let go of the badge which subsequently caused the badge to retract quickly. This not only was a visual distraction but it became an auditory distraction due to the sound it made when it snapped back into place. To make matters worse, this particular trainer endangered the heads and eyes of the audience because he took his "badge retraction skills" to a new level.

He began extending the badge to its furthest point, then began to spin the string that held the badge around his finger. Think of a coach twirling his whistle around his finger repeatedly at practice. This caused concern of the audience because they began leaning away from the trainer because they were worried they'd be hit in the face by the badge hurling through the air.

Not a great experience for the audience.

Now that we've identified some of the common nervous habits that rear their ugly heads during sessions, let's explore how we take the necessary steps to overcome them.

Overcoming Nervous Habits

First and foremost, the best thing to help keep your nerves at bay is to breathe. As rudimentary as that sounds since we all must breathe to survive, it is important to control how we are breathing.

When we get nervous, our heart rate increases, which can shorten our breaths. This subsequently can drive tension throughout the body. Focusing on your ability to efficiently breathe will help you remain calm and connected with the task at hand, which is delivering an exceptional experience.

The silliest thing about nervous habits is they can appear, and we have no idea we are doing it. This is where having someone to observe you can be valuable.

An example where an observer was valuable for me came when I was co-facilitating a presentation skills class. I picked up a distractive habit that I had no idea was there until the session was over. My colleague pointed out that every time after I gestured with my hands, my hands inadvertently smacked the side of my legs. Even though it wasn't necessarily from nerves, it became an audible distraction due to the high volume.

Now that I was aware of this, my quick fix was to be mindful of how I was bringing my hands back down to my side. I made sure that instead of palms hitting my legs when I brought my hands down, I subtly turned my palms toward the audience so the outside of my hand (pinky side) would make contact, which completely mitigated the audible distraction.

When nerves begin to kick in and the tension throughout the body, namely in the shoulders and neck areas, as mentioned, controlling your breath will be valuable, and to aid in relaxing is focusing on your ability to slightly slow your rate of speech.

Too many times I have seen presenters/facilitators get so nervous, their rate of speech increases. What occurs at this point is now your brain and mouth are not in sync. This leads to the situation of saying something in front of an audience you didn't intend.

Now I am not trying to tell you that your rate of speech needs to crawl along at a turtle's pace, but deceleration of word volume can be vital. For anyone that may have driven a manual transmission vehicle. These are vehicles that have a stick shift where the driver has to manually move to different gears to reach higher or lower speeds. If you find your words are flowing out of mouth at a high rate of speed, think of this as being in 5th gear (commonly the highest gear). If you are in this gear, your words are traveling as quickly as a vehicle traveling 50+ miles per hour. Just like in vehicles, the faster you are moving, this increases your chances for catastrophic events.

This is where downshifting can be so valuable. By simply downshifting to a lower gear, namely 4th gear, you maintain a good rate of speed but now you are in more control of the vehicle. The same applies when you're speaking.

Slightly downshifting to maintain control of the words exiting your face keeps you in control and avoids disaster.

With the examples of fiddling with accessories, this is VERY simple. Get rid of the accessory.

Don't take me literally in that recommendation. I don't want you to throw your badge away, as I'd imagine you'd like to be able to navigate your company's building successfully. I also don't want you to take your jewelry box and dump the contents into the dumpster.

This can be as simple as removing the items before your session starts.

When I think of badges, I usually don't think of my badge once it is attached to my belt, when I've needed to wear one. However, to not only avoid the temptation, I also remove it to prevent is swaying back and forth during the session and it becoming a visual distraction for the audience. My best practice is to place it in my bag, preferably somewhere easily accessible for breaks.

The same applies for jewelry. Take it off, or an even better approach, plan ahead and don't wear loose jewelry. Most people if they have jewelry would prefer not to leave jewelry in their bag or on a table due to sentimental reasons. I get that. Just plan ahead and avoid the situation.

When you think about your hair, similar rules apply. If you have longer hair, keep it up or neatly out of your face. This can help avoid the temptation.

A former colleague, and an exceptional facilitator, would always tell me that no matter what, she would never wear her hair down when she was training a class. She did this for a couple reasons. It not only prevented the temptation of fiddling with it, but she is a proponent of a clean, professional look when she was in front of an audience. This ties wonderfully to the next section around appearance.

Anxiety going into a session can and will usually occur with a lack of preparation. Take the necessary steps to prepare. In the next category, we will dive deeply into how to best prepare for sessions, but it is important to know the lack of preparation feeds the "anxiety monster." What can occur is you will likely spend more time worried about not knowing what you need to achieve in your session. Even if you have delivered a particular session hundreds of times, if you are not fully prepared, there will be nerves that surface. This can show up as stress in front of your audience, which then minimizes your ability to deliver an exceptional experience.

There have been situations when I didn't adequately prepare for a session and it didn't create the seamless environment I preferred to deliver. One example is when I traveled to a location to facilitate a class. I took for granted that I'd been to this location before, I was familiar with the content, so I didn't follow my usual protocol for waking up at the right time to arrive on site at my usual time. When I arrived, the room was in disorder and the supplies I assumed were in the room, were not there. I began scrambling to locate the easel sheets I needed to place on the wall ahead of time. In addition, I had to pick up the room and put the room back in order (e.g. aligning tables, pushing chairs in). I had only been in the room fifteen minutes and the learners started to arrive. This led to my stress level increasing because they were seeing a lot of the behind the scenes work that I prefer to have remedied before learners arrive. As the start time moved closer, my stress level increased. I attempted to hide my stress but due to the increased stress level, my opening wasn't as strong as it needed to be so I then had to work that much harder throughout the day to overcome the less than stellar start. Not to mention the additional filler words that creeped in throughout that below standard opening I delivered.

Getting over nerves in front of an audience takes repetition, or practice. These practice reps can occur with the number of times you deliver a particular session, whether it's a session with an actual audience or even by yourself.

Are you familiar with the "3 Ps" of practice?

Practice. Practice. Practice.

Creating the "muscle memory" with your delivery can aid in your ability to overcome nerves. Prescribing a specific way to practice is tough because each of you are different in knowing what it takes for you to feel comfortable with the content.

I've had facilitators/presenters share some of their best practices for practicing:

- Co-facilitate a session with a facilitator that has delivered the content previously,
- Read the content aloud,
- Write out all the speaking points verbatim 1-3 times,
- Deliver the content in front of a mirror,
- Deliver the content to a cat.

This last one may sound somewhat outlandish, yet for the person that shared it mentioned this is what worked for her. Which is fantastic. The reps were there, that is the most important part.

For me, when I was pursuing my Speech Communications degree at Colorado State University, I realized that if I wanted to shake some of my nervous energy that was showing up, I decided to take an elective course in Acting. It was an entry level class, but it was amazingly helpful. When we were delivering a scene of our own creation, I decided come out in front of the class in just a towel, as I wanted to set the scene that I was just out of the shower. It was at that moment that figured, if I can get up in front of a room full of classmates wearing only a towel, I could get in front of any audience.

Please note, I am not encouraging you to go out on stage in a towel, but if you push yourself outside your comfort zone, you will smash through your nervous barriers.

Appearance

The last element in the Confidence category is appearance. This particular element is one that has been one of the most contested concepts I've encountered throughout my career.

Let's start with a baseline standard. When you are getting ready to deliver a session, the standard I have always upheld has been **dress at least one level above your audience.**

The reason this has been contested is I have had facilitators/presenters mention "this takes away from who I am" or "it doesn't matter how I am dressed because the group is focused on my content."

Both are reasonable perspectives. However, the intent for this standard isn't to dictate how someone should dress.

The purpose of dressing one level above your audience is to show respect to your audience. They are taking time to be part of your session and it is an indirect way to appreciate their time away from how they make money or time away from their family. It is not intended to demonstrate a level of superiority.

Think about this, if you into two different classrooms, one instructor is wearing shorts and a t-shirt and the other is wearing a suit, your initial reaction is likely to want to listen to the one wearing a suit. The person wearing a suit makes an immediate impact on you at a higher level of credibility as a professional because of the care they put into their attire.

It is completely possible that the person wearing the shorts and a t-shirt is a marvelous facilitator/presenter and the one wearing the suit is a dud. The importance is we only have a few seconds to make a great first impression when we first encounter someone. The person wearing the shorts and t-shirt would have to work harder to demonstrate credibility to overcome that initial first impression.

When it comes to delivering a session, your appearance can be an immediate credibility builder.

One of the best demonstrations of this came when I was in college. I had a professor in one of my media communications classes that was talking through the value of appearance. On this particular day, he showed up to class in a suit, which wasn't his norm to wear a full suit. However, this is where it became interesting. When he began discussing the value of how you appear, especially in media, he asked the question, "if I am wearing this, how likely are you to listen to me?" The entire class nodded positively acknowledging his point.

Then, he took off his suit coat and repeated the question, again the class all agreed that we'd be willing to listen. He then took off his tie, repeating his question. Again, with the class reaffirming our prior positive acknowledgments. Upon the additional positive reaction from the class, he removed his dress shirt and shoes, leaving him in his slacks and undershirt. Of course, giggles ensued from the class, but the reactions changed from positive affirmations to more of a "meh" reaction from the class.

Lastly, he dropped his pants. This left him standing in front of a class of college aged students wearing nothing but an undershirt and boxer shorts. Not only could you hear a pin drop, but with the number of mouths left agape in the room, a swarm of flies could've taken residency in the open caverns. He repeated his question again and this time the class shook their heads in absolute disagreement.

The point my professor was making is the value of perception and gaining immediate buy-in before any words are uttered.

So, as you think about your appearance, think about these two questions:

- What perception do you want to portray?
- What is the impression you want to make?

With the right frame of mind, and knowing our appearance plays a huge factor in gaining initial credibility, we need to explore what to consider for our appearance.

Business casual should be a minimum. How you dress sets the tone for your day. If you are dressed too casually, your performance will follow.

Early in my career, I was part of an exercise on the impact dress can have on performance. Shortly after I graduated, I left a good job because I had a disagreement with my boss. It was a knee jerk reaction that many of have made when we were early in our career. My girlfriend, who eventually became my wife, told me since we were living together, that I had 30 days before things got too tight for us financially. I eventually ended up taking a call center job at a satellite tv provider. Not the most glamorous job, but I would not trade that experience for the world. When I started, the attire standard at the call center was business casual. Pretty much it was a nice shirt and pants that weren't jeans. After being there for two weeks, our center made the employee friendly decision to all casual dress as a trial. As a young person, I was so excited. I got to wear shorts to work.

This trial did not go as planned. Call quality dropped significantly. The biggest component of this was due to the fact that everyone talking to customers presented themselves like they were dressed. If you are unfamiliar, in the call center environment, call quality is one of the biggest factors for call center success. I have to give credit to the centers leadership, at the end of the trial they outlined what happened and explained why we couldn't be fully casual.

Although this is not related to being in front of an audience, it was a lesson I never forgot. I have carried that lesson with me throughout my career.

You carry yourself more confidently if you feel good about how you are dressed. I know when I put on a suit, I feel amazing. I know from the women I've worked with, and even my wife, when they have that outfit that looks good and it fits the way they want it, they feel amazing.

Now consider the image you portray to your audience when you feel confident and look good, your audience will notice and sense that energy.

If business casual is the starting point, managing color schemes plays a valuable role as well. You want to ensure things match.

Trust me, if things don't match, that will be the day you have a fashionista in your audience that is unable to look at you because things don't match. This also applies with the colors you choose. If you showed up to a session wearing red pants and a yellow shirt, I guarantee you that your audience won't be thinking about your confidence level, they will be wondering why you look like condiments.

Black is a safe color. It is a safe color and many folks like how they look in black. Grey is pretty safe as well. It can be helpful to add some color. For instance, if I wear a suit for a session, I usually go with a black, grey, or blue suit, but I will add a tie that has color. It is a good accent piece.

For women, I've seen wonderful examples where a colorful scarf is worn to add a little color. Women also have used jewelry to accent their look and add color to their ensemble.

Here is point of clarification to this baseline of dressing one level above your audience. It should be just that, one level above. The reason this is pertinent is if you are going into a company that has a very relaxed attire standard as part of their culture, think of the early days in tech start-ups, like Google. People were afforded the opportunity to wear what they wanted and anyone that walked in wearing a suit immediately were discounted because they didn't fit in. A former colleague of mine told me a story that a friend of theirs went to one of these tech start-ups to train a class wearing a suit. Before he was allowed to get past security, he was told he needed to take off his suit jacket and lose the tie.

If you find yourself in one of those situations, find a bit of a balance. Perhaps you wear jeans with a sport coat. Possibly just slacks and a polo shirt. This still allows you to demonstrate a level of respect to your audience while aligning a little more closely to the culture you are entering.

On the opposite side of the spectrum, this does not mean that if you are delivering a session to a room full of executives with suits and ties that you need to wear full formal gear (e.g. tuxedo). Wearing attire that is business formal (men=suit and tie of basic colors; women=pants suit or business dress) will aid in showing the respect for the audience while aligning culturally.

The last element that comes with appearance is around watches. If you are a wearer of watches make sure it remains as an accessory and not a focal point.

Try something for me.

Stand up and let your arms hang to your sides. Even if you are not wearing a watch, act as if you are checking the time.

It was a pretty significant arm movement upward, correct? You're bringing your arm up, which is a large arm movement, and your head looks down to see the time.

Similar to the contagious nature of smiles, if you check the time in front of your audience, your audience will as well. This can lead to their minds starting to wander, "Is it almost break time?" "How much longer do we have?"

This is important because I've worked with a people that love watches and they like the style of them. It is viewed by some that it is more than just a time piece, it is a fashion statement. However, it can also be a distraction.

One of the ultimate ninja tricks I learned long ago was to place the watch face on the inside of your wrist. Then, as you're looking at your notes, you can take note of the time without drawing attention to the time.

This subtle nuance keeps your appearance intact and it allows your audience to remain focused on what is being covered.

All of the elements, even the most minute ones, covered for the category of Confidence are intentional to put you into the ideal state to be the most confident version of yourself, which then positions you to keep your audience bought into you and drives an enhanced level of credibility, even before you start your session.

7

PREPARATION

Self

Preparation is valuable and yet anytime I've trained a presentation skills or a trainer certification class, when we brainstorm ideas on preparation, very rarely does a participant mention self-preparation.

It is the most overlooked component of preparation yet one of the most impactful. Which is why I am starting with it.

Imagine you have every piece of material for a session, all your technology works, the audience is smiling as they walk in, everything is ready for a great session, BUT you aren't quite feeling it. Perhaps you have a bit of a foggy brain, you're tired, you feel like you're moving slower than normal. With all of those dynamics in place, how good do you think your session will be?

If you answered, "not a good one." You'd be right.

You as the presenter/facilitator, you are the engine that runs the "session vehicle." Without the engine, a car doesn't go anywhere. It may look pretty, but it's not going anywhere without that engine.

PREPARATION

This means the natural proclivity to ensure all the ancillary items (e.g. technology, presentation slides) are ready to go and working normally, none of that works if you are not prepared.

Here are some self-preparation concepts that have worked well for me.

Hydrate

Being at the right hydration level will be crucial. You will be moving and speaking a lot during your session. You are exerting energy, which means your body will function better if it is adequately hydrated.

You will also want to balance it so you aren't overly hydrated causing you to do the "pee pee" dance in front of your audience. Even though the audience won't mind additional breaks, it reduces your session run time, which could impact your goal of achieving your objective(s) for the session in the allotted timeframe.

On average I consume about one gallon of water per day. Of course, there is a bit of an ebb and flow to that number depending on what is going on during the day, but that is about average.

Starting your day, immediately upon waking, with 30 oz of water gets you out of the dehydration mode that occurs while you're sleeping. If drinking water is not a common practice for you, this may sound like a lot. However, this can be a good starting point to start building the habit to ensure you are fully hydrated for your session.

There are supplements on the market that are quality supplements to help you remain hydrated. Nuun is my go-to electrolyte supplement, especially because it does not have high sugar content. I will utilize these tablets that dissolve in water to help increase my hydration level, especially on days I am leading a session and I know I won't get as much water.

Eating

Quick disclaimer, I am not a dietician or nutritionist, so what I'm sharing with you here is based solely on what works for me.

Although this may sound basic, but the wrong meal can make you sluggish, especially coming back from lunch if you're running a full day session.

My practice is to utilize Dr. Shawn Baker's carnivore diet strategies consistently; this helps me remain satisfied and prevents hunger pains.

For me personally, the higher protein levels have been a staple for me due to the years I have spent working out and competing in strength sports. This has translated well when I lead session. By minimizing sugar and consuming higher proteins it enhances how I function when leading a class.

This is not intended to make you completely change your dietary habits, it is mentioned because what you consume is important to ensuring you are optimized for success for delivering sessions and something not to be overlooked.

There may be a little bit of trial and error on your part to gauge how you feel after consuming certain meal types. Based on my personal experience and my own trial and error, you should get sense of how well your meal is working for you approximately 60-120 minutes after you've consumed the meal.

Do you feel hungry or are you adequately satiated?

Do you feel an energy crash or is your energy sustained?

Do you feel your mind wandering or are you able to remain focused?

Pay attention to how you are feeling, it can make a difference. Listening to your body will help ensure you are optimized for sustained success.

Caffeinate

We've heard the old adage, "don't talk to me before I've had my morning coffee." It is humorous as caffeine can help us wake up in the morning and start the day anew. Caffeine is helpful to pick us up when we feel sluggish, or when we've had really long days.

There are numerous options available that have caffeine. Supplements. Coffee. Energy Drinks. Tea. If someone has a proclivity toward caffeine they have their preferred caffeine delivery mechanism.

Caffeine has been a staple for me, and I have consumed caffeine products for several years. Black coffee (no cream or sugar) and zero sugar energy drinks are my preferred caffeine mechanisms. I have found them to provide the energy I need, when I need it. The important call-out is the zero sugar. I have found that the added sugar makes me feel more sluggish and drives a faster drop/crash sooner. Which is not something I need when I'm in front of an audience.

I mention this element in Self Preparation because I accept it is valuable for me and many others I've worked with.

HOWEVER!

It is also highly important that you know your tolerance level. Know what levels work for you before you board the caffeine train, especially leading up to a session.

This was something I never thought of until I was co-facilitating with a colleague and good friend. We were training a trainer certification class in Greeley, CO and on our way back from grabbing lunch, I asked if we could stop by a convenience store so I could pick up a Sugar-Free Red Bull. While in the store, my colleague mentioned, I think I'll try one, I've never had one before. This should've been a red flag.

We make our way back to the office and when we reconvened, he was covering the module right after lunch. He began the module and was doing really well. Until.

He was approximately 15 minutes into the module and as I sat in the back of the room, I happened to notice his rate of speech began increasing. Faster and faster and faster. I began to see him visibly sweating too.

Seeing this freight train building up speed, I nonchalantly raised my hand from the back of the room and asked if I could add something to what he mentioned. I had a feeling he needed a lifeline.

As the class turned to look at him in the back, I saw him immediately bend over and put his hands on his knees. He began taking very deep breaths. I knew he needed to catch his breath. So, I began vamping to buy him some time until he could catch his breath and slow down.

He and I laugh about it to this day and to quote him, "I felt my heart beating through my teeth. I am never drinking that shit again."

As humorous as it is in hindsight, I mention it because caffeine can be helpful, but it is vital that if you board the caffeine train, you need to know what your body can tolerate.

Sleep

I've learned the hard way, especially if I am traveling to train a class or deliver a presentation, that sleep impacts the quality of a session. The impact can be positive if I get a good night's rest, and a negative impact with less.

My personal sleep target is 7 hours every night. At the time of writing this book, I have two young boys with mountains of energy, two German Shepherds under the age of three that crave early morning walks, a full-time job, a side hustle, and a wife I enjoy spending time with even in small windows around the busy schedules.

The above is not highlighted to show I am busy. I mention it because as I've started writing this book and training classes on top of everything listed, the importance of good sleep has never been more important.

Life likes to throw curveballs at us all. Life does not worry about if you have a session you need to deliver.

When you have a session coming up, sleep should be prioritized. Block the time. Give yourself a bedtime and commit to the fact that you will be in bed by a certain time.

Have I trained classes with approximately three hours of sleep? Yes.

Was I heavily caffeinated going into those sessions? You better believe it.

Making it through a session that is less than a day, it is possible to deliver a quality short session on one poor night of sleep. Where it has caught up to me is if I am delivering a class that is multiple days. If I don't get good sleep before the first day, I know that starting on day 2, my session will be impacted by that poor first night of sleep.

Everyone may be different, but minimal sleep doesn't hit me until the day after. So, if I sleep poorly on a Sunday night, I will feel the effects Tuesday.

By getting a good night's sleep before your session, helps reduce stress, focuses your mind, and allows you to have the necessary energy levels when it's showtime.

Shower (Hot or Cold)

Nothing beats a good shower. You feel refreshed. You feel clean. Ensuring that I start my session feeling refreshed is valuable for me.

Most folks prefer warm or hot showers. It's comfortable. Yet, if I really want to get my day off to a highly energetic start, I will take a normal shower, and then in the last couple minutes of my shower, I will turn the water as cold as I can. This immediately activates the senses. It is brutal if it is something in which you're not accustomed, however the immediate bolt of energy that shoots through your system is exhilarating.

Calling out showers as part of the self-preparation may seem rudimentary, and it is. However, the negative ramifications are hard to rebound from.

There was a trainer I worked with that was based in Arkansas. When I arrived onsite, I was making my rounds and I stopped into his class to observe for a couple minutes. Not only was this trainer sitting down at the desk in front of the room while going through his PowerPoint, but he had his feet up on the desk. He was dressed in all black, made up of a t-shirt, cargo pants, and combat boots. He was also wearing a black trench coat. This was not the worst of it, when he sent the class to a break, it was evident that he hadn't showered in what smelled like a couple days.

There were several compounding issues with that situation, but the most unfortunate one was because he had an unpleasant aroma, which smelled like cigarette smoke and body odor. Just by observing the body language of the class, they preferred him to stay at the front of the class, so they didn't have to smell him. It was an immediate credibility killer.

Warming Up

When it is cold outside and you have to go somewhere there are likely two thoughts that cross your mind, bundle up and start the car. You add layers of clothes to keep you warm and you start the car to warm it up. It is rough climbing into a cold car. In order for the car to heat up and provide good heat to keep you warm, it needs to warm up itself.

The same applies to you.

You are like a machine.

Like most machines you need to warm up to perform optimally.

As a presenter/facilitator, your voice is your most powerful tool. To begin priming my voice, I will usually drink a warm drink. My preference is coffee, however tea or warm water work just as well. The warm drink allows your physical voice elements (e.g. throat, voice box) to be warm and loose. Cold drinks are refreshing but when it comes time for warm up the voice, I've found they provide a feeling of tightness and rigidity. The warm drink also allows me to gain more resonance in the deeper registers of my vocal range.

After drinking my warm drink, I sing. It is important to note, I am not a great singer, but I sing my heart out. If I am driving to a location to train or present, the entire drive I am singing. I created a playlist of songs that test my vocal range and are of moderate tempo so I can focus getting the various points of my vocal range. I focus more on the lower registers (deep voice) as it helps my voice muscles continue to flex. My playlist consists of music from Frank Sinatra, The Eagles, After 7, Boyz II Men, and Darius Rucker.

My body is another area I work to warm-up. To help ensure I can make it through a full session, I have to get moving. I make sure I get some sort of exercise as soon as I wake up. Usually a 30-45 walk, preferably outside. Depending on the time of my session I am delivering, I may include some strength training. This has been as simple as doing 100 push-ups before I eat breakfast. The act of getting moving allows me to get the blood flowing.

About an hour before the session, I take more targeted physical actions. This starts with my face.

Not only do I increase my facial expressions while singing (extra facial animation), I conduct extra steps before the session. The main exercise I do to help warm up my face is doing the Lemon Face/Tiger Face exercise. I do this exercise to flex my facial muscles before a session. This allows my facial muscles to be more pliable, which increases my ability to be more expressive with my face during a session.

Here's how I do it:

While standing, start with the tiger face, which is widening the eyes, opening the mouth as wide as possible, raising the eyebrows to their highest peak.

- I will even get my hands involved by making my hands like tiger claws about shoulder height.

PREPARATION

I immediately switch to lemon face, this is scrunching everything as tight as possible, as if you just ate a lemon; squinting eyes tightly, closing mouth and pursing lips tightly, and furrowing the brow.

- Keeping my hands involved, I will pull all my fingers together into a one point.

You will feel REALLY silly doing this exercise, but after you do it a couple times, you will feel the difference in the flexibility of your facial muscles.

I also try to smile as much as possible. This is priming my brain to avoid my natural tendency of being in RBF (Resting Bitch Face). In the next section, Refocus Your Mind, I will cover ideas how I smile more before a session.

This indirect training essentially places your brain in a positive, upbeat mindset. This practice helps even before the session starts when you're smiling while greeting participants.

There can be a lot that goes into self-preparation and it will be something that is specific to you. It will take some time to find what works best for you.

Refocus Your Mind

Transitioning from daily life, both personal and professional, into delivering an exceptional session can have some difficulties. As previously mentioned, Being Present and utilizing your little red wagon can help. Yet, here's where the difficulty lies.

You may be a master at separating yourself from outside "noise" in your life before you walk into a session, which is amazing. The downside is if you have heavy life stuff weighing you down before you walk into a session, your head is still in whatever state it was in before you walked into the room.

I had an instance with a class I was training that took its toll on my headspace and it was difficult to separate from.

I was scheduled to deliver a leadership development class for a group of managers outside of the Dallas/Fort Worth area in Texas. It was during a time when this particular location was moving from its initial temporary building into the new complex that recently opened. Unfortunately, the training rooms at the new complex were not fully ready, so we had to do the class in the old temporary building, which many of the attendees had to drive to from the new complex. In addition, there was a skeleton crew still operating at the building. This meant that the support groups, namely the cafeteria, had minimal staff.

Here's where my headspace went astray. During this session, we committed to providing the class with lunch that would be set up by the cafeteria staff at the time arranged by our training coordinator. As we got closer to breaking for lunch, I continued to look to see where the food was set up. Nothing. During the last activity, I reached out to the coordinator inquiring about lunch and where it was going to be set up. When it was time to break for lunch, I checked my messages, and the coordinator confirmed the cafeteria staff never delivered the lunch and never planned to fill the order.

This is where the big vein in my forehead began to pulsate. Since we committed to providing lunch for the class, I took the entire class of over 20 people into the café at lunch time and had them create a line as we ordered each of their individual lunches at the kiosk. As you can imagine, the lunch time needed to be extended by 30 minutes to allow for the food to be prepared for each person and allow time for everyone to eat.

I was highly frustrated. Now our timeframe for the afternoon was compressed and the experience for the group was not as seamless as it was supposed to be. Although I attempted to fake positivity for the rest of the afternoon and brush it off, in my head, I was still stewing. Due to this, the session was impacted and I knew I didn't deliver the best afternoon I should have for the learners.

I knew better than to let something like that hijack my headspace, yet it did.

This is why it is important to get your mind right before you start delivering a session.

Here are some concepts that have helped me throughout the years ensure I don't get stuck in the trap of letting outside situations invade my headspace and my head is focused on the aligned environment I want to create.

My ideal headspace going into a session is energetic and positive. It doesn't take much for me to get there because I love engaging with an audience. To help cement that flow into my mind going into a session is I watch humorous shows. My go-to's are tv sitcoms and stand-up comedy.

I grew up watching sitcoms, including reruns from the 1950s and 1960s. For whatever reason I gravitated toward these types of shows. Watching a favorite good classic sitcom is something I have always enjoyed.

Some of my all-time favorite sitcoms:

PREPARATION

- *Rules of Engagement*
- *Big Bang Theory*
- *Three's Company*
- *Happy Day*

The other device I incorporate to get my mind in the right space are stand-up comedies. I am not sure how or when I got hooked on good stand-up comedy, but I have always enjoyed them. As I grew into the profession of presenting and facilitating, I found a great deal of correlation between oration and stand-up comedy.

Think about it. Both require strong stage presence, effective delivery of material, and creating exceptional experiences. Watching clips from some of my favorite comedians makes me laugh, even if I've watched the same routine several times and even though I know what the punchline is that approaching, it is always entertaining. The comedians whose specials I have watched the most through the years are John PInette and Tim Allen.

Of course, every person on this blue marble that's hurling through space (earth) have their own preferences as to what they find funny. I have had former colleagues tell me they like my sense of humor, yet if you ask my wife, I am not funny at all.

My usual process for utilizing these tools to my advantage is I will usually watch a couple good sitcoms the night before a session. Then the morning of a session, while I am getting ready, I will watch a standup comedy. This way, before I fall asleep, I am priming my brain and then I am reinforcing that mindset right before.

If you 're not a fan of TV like I am, and reading is more your style, think of things that are uplifting for you. It could be a good book that makes you giggle or even reading something uplifting can be valuable. The goal is to get you into a positive frame of mind.

A word of caution I would offer is to avoid "dark" content before a session. These types of shows or books can have the opposite effect on your frame of mind. I learned this lesson the hard way.

I'd heard a lot of great feedback from friends about the hit show "Sons of Anarchy." If you haven't heard about this show, it is a show about a motorcycle gang in California. The show centered around the dark life (e.g. drugs and murder) of a fictional motorcycle gang. After it had been out for a few years, I decided to begin watching the show. I definitely got caught up into the show. Unknowingly, I found myself going into sessions I was training during this time with a very cynical mindset. There were times I was constantly thinking what the motives were of those in the session, assuming it was with ill intent, even if it was a simple question they had about the content. These classes weren't as strong as I'd hoped. It took a lot of self-reflection to come this unfortunate realization.

Materials

The materials or content that will be part of your session should be prepared ahead of time. Even the most gifted of presenters and facilitators, don't go into session "cold" by not preparing their materials or content ahead of time. It is part of the work that goes on behind the scenes that makes great sessions.

A best practice I learned early in my journey of delivering sessions is to review the next days content the night before, even if I'd delivered it several times before.

If you have trained the content many times before, it may not have to be a full granular content review. The intent behind this is it brings the content for the next day to the forefront of your mind. I have found this to be extremely valuable doing it the night before because it allows my brain to be thinking about it even while I sleep. Doing this review the night before has put me into a position that I am thinking about it first thing in the morning.

Reviewing the content the night before is essentially one of the last content reviews you may have and if you are getting ready to deliver content you've never delivered before there is quite a bit of work that needs to be done leading up to that point.

If I am preparing for content I've never delivered before I start reviewing the content at least two weeks before. Depending on the course, there may be a "train-the-trainer" session, which is an observation of the session by someone who has delivered the content previously. The "train-the-trainer" is valuable because you can get a sense of how the class flows, you can observe how the activities are designed, and how the media/technology supports the training.

When I am facilitating a training, the weeks leading up to a session, I will read through the content, usually the Facilitator Guide. I developed a process that helps me capture key points and makes it easy to reference while in front of a class. It is the magnificent usage of highlighters.

When I am doing my highlights, I stick to FOUR colors, and only four colors:

- Green – highlights for questions to be asked
- Pink – highlights key important points
- Yellow – highlights activities to be facilitated
- Blue – highlights trainer call-outs (e.g. trainer demonstration)

This strategy has helped me systematize my preparation and it creates visual cues that are easily referenced while delivering a training. The highlighter colors have trained my brain to recognize in the moment things that need to be covered. It also prevents me from having to read a section while in front of an audience. At least for me, it feels like an awkward moment when I am in front of a class, and I am staring at my notes or guide trying to extract information that needs to be conveyed.

When I am presenting, usually these are situations when I won't have notes in my hand, so the highlighter cues don't translate. However, when I have been on stage delivering a presentation, I have found different workarounds.

Depending on the size of the presentation, if you are on a stage, and your visuals are on a screen behind you, there are commonly confidence monitors at the front of the stage that can you look down quickly to see the slides and any talking points that would normally show up in the notes portion of a PowerPoint.

In these notes sections, I will bold key words as the primary visual anchor for me. This has helped me because as I am practicing my presentation, I work to utilize the bold words so I can quickly reference.

I think of these like signs along the highway. If you are driving in an area in which you are unfamiliar, you will utilize the signs (e.g. exit ramps and distance to destination) to aid in your navigation. I also use these signs to ensure I am still going in the right direction toward my destination. The bold words serve the same purpose for me as I am presenting in front of an audience. They are quick indicators to ensure I am on track.

Occasionally, I will underline certain words, but depending on the size of the confidence monitors, or if your confidence monitor is your laptop screen, seeing an underlined word may be tough.

Audience Materials

The materials that are provided to the audience need to be ready no later than the day before. If you are waiting until the day of your session to get audience materials ready, you are likely putting yourself into a position of higher stress and anxiety that can be prevented. As you are seeing there is a lot that goes into preparing for a session, especially the day of. Adding an element that can be planned for is getting you too close to not delivering your best possible session.

You're likely wondering, "All I have to do is print off 20 guides."

That may be true. And those guides may only be a couple pages long. But what if your printer goes down? What if the printer runs out of ink? What if you run out of staples and you can't find paperclips? What if you planned to print them out before class when you arrive an hour before your session, but there's an accident and you are delayed arriving at the location of your session?"

We could play the "What If" game until we both want to take a long walk off a short pier, yet my point is even those little circumstances can and will happen. It takes planning.

Even the most random minute circumstances can have maddening ramifications.

I had a situation where I was scheduled to deliver leadership class in San Francisco and participant kits were sent from the content vendor. I had checked all the boxes in preparation. I received confirmation from the coordinator that the materials arrived in the building three days in advance. The class was scheduled to start at 8am and I arrived a little before 7am. I arrived in the training room and started to get situated. Now I needed to go to the desk of the person that received the materials. At this company, there are several floors occupied. I had to visit several floors to attempt to find the person's desk. After walking through multiple floors, I finally found the box. Just one box, when there should've been at least two.

To make matters worse because the class started at 8am, I was in the office before anyone else, especially anyone that could aid me in trying to track down the other box. Ultimately, after 30 minutes of wandering, I made it back to the training room and less than half of the kits were found. I ended up having to cancel the class as people were coming in because we needed a minimum of eight people to deliver the class, based on the design of the content, and we only had six participant kits. To make matters worse, there were three people that traveled in to attend this class along with other meetings. It was certainly the one of the most embarrassing situations I've ever had with an audience.

In the end, we did end up getting those scheduled for this canceled class into another session and prioritized their attendance for when it worked best for their schedule. It was important that we did everything we could to try to make up for the situation they had no control over.

Visual Aids

These are the various items that are part of a training or presentation. The most common visual aids that are not technology related (e.g. PowerPoint), are easel sheets.

I am a fan of easel sheets. I wouldn't say I create the best-looking easel sheets when I am using them during a session, due to my lackluster art skills and brutal handwriting, but I love using them. They are so fun to drive engagement with an audience and can change up the visual elements that are part of your delivery. Thusly shifting, even for a short period, away from a dependency on PowerPoint.

PREPARATION

To put you in a position to utilize these to the highest value, there are some common mishaps that occur and can easily be overcome with preparation:

Mishap #1 - Not preparing the easel sheets ahead of time.

Far too often trainers will only utilize easel sheets as a last resort or only think about using them when the time comes to capture ideas. Then when it's time, they grab a blank sheet and advise the audience to start throwing out responses to a question.

To overcome this mishap, by reviewing your material the night before, you remind yourself how many instances the next day that you need easel sheets. When arriving the next day, ensure you prepare your sheets. One of the most helpful facilitator guides I've used contained a quick "set-up" sheet at the beginning of each days content, which included the easel sheets that needed to be prepared for the day.

Overcoming Mishap #1:

- **Add a title** - this helps focus the attention of the audience and makes it easier for future reference.
- **Add a border** - a border of some type helps draw the attention of the audience into the sheet, especially if you post the sheet on the wall.
- **Only use 2-3 colors per sheet** - the color variety makes the sheet more visually appealing but limiting the colors avoids it from being too overwhelming. Dark colors (black, green, blue) are ideal to ensure it's visible.

Mishap #2 - Making prepared easel sheets visible before they're needed

If you are in a position and you have prepared easel sheets ahead of time, this common mistake usually comes after all the easels sheets are prepared and posted throughout the room. This becomes a visual distraction for the learners. In addition, it takes away the element of surprise.

The element of surprise is powerful tool for presenters/facilitators because it helps control where the audience focuses. There have been instances where I've seen trainers post their prepared easel sheets throughout the room and then out of curiosity, the class begins asking questions about what they mean, or when that will be covered. It is our job as the presenter/facilitator to control the timing of the message.

Overcoming Mishap #2:

- **Keep them hidden** – if you post the easels on a wall, take a blank sheet and place it over the top, so all the audience sees is a blank sheet.
- **Move the stand** – if you are not posting the sheets on a wall and have your sheets on an easel stand, keep the sheets hidden, but also move the stand out of the main view of the audience until it is needed. Then you can move it into the main focus (e.g. front/center of the room)

I've even gone so far to place the easel stand in the back of the room and when I need it, I move to the back of the room which shifts the focus of the audience and adds more movement area for me. Win/win.

Mishap #3 - Forget the location of the easel sheets

It is humorous when it happens to someone else, yet it is insanely frustrating when it happens to you. Forgetting where you placed your prepared easel sheet is awkward. It could be if you placed it on the wall and covered with a blank sheet and you forget which is which. The other situation is if you prepare your easel sheets ahead of time and keep them within the full pad and forget where within the pad, the specific easel sheet is located. Either scenario negatively impacts the flow of your session.

PREPARATION

Overcoming Mishap #3:

- **Place them in order on the wall** - when you place them on the wall start at one point, then put them in sequential order rotating around the room. This allows you to know the first one starts here and then when it is time for the next one, you can go right to it.

Ninja tip: you can also place a discreet number, preferably with a pen or pencil, on the blank sheet in one of the corners so you can glance quickly when you are close to it to know which one it is.

- **Paper Clips & Dog Ears** - if you keep your easels within the original pad together, you can place paper clips on the side closest to you to you easily grab the sheets before and flip right to the page you need. You can also "dog ear" the lower corner of the page before it.

This also prevents the weird scenario of flipping multiple sheets, one after the other, to get to the one you need. Flip multiple sheets at the same time. Done.

Mishap #4 - "What does it say behind there?"

This is the question that can occur if multiple sheets are stacked against each other in succession. Inevitably, the colorful text can be seen yet somewhat indecipherable. This can lead to the audience having a harder time reading what you are listing or driving their curiosity to what is behind that sheet. Which takes away from the task at hand.

Overcoming Mishap #4:

- **Keep a blank sheet in between** - when preparing your easels ahead of time, be sure to leave at least one blank sheet between each prepared easel sheet. This will eliminate a potential distraction.

Mishap #5 - Training or presenting to the sheet

This is not a common thought for facilitators or presenters when they are using easel sheets, or even dry erase boards. As they begin capturing ideas, they will talk while they are writing.

When I've trained classes in Central America and the Philippines, they view this as a "no-no" as well because it is turning your back to the audience. Which can be a good practice, yet tough to do sometimes when you need to be in a better position to write.

The key is to avoid is making it seem like you are talking to the inanimate object.

In addition, by doing this, it can also minimize the audiences ability to hear you, especially those in the back of the room.

Overcoming Mishap #5:

- **Write, then finish your thought** - this one can be uncomfortable for some facilitators and presenters. By writing without speaking places silence in the room which can feel awkward for some. It only is for a few seconds to capture what you need, then face the audience and add your commentary.
- **Write sideways** - by doing this, you have the ability to still face the audience while writing and additional commentary can be added.

Here's how it works:

1. If you are left-handed (like I am), you will stand to the side of the easel and you will keep your right foot pointed to the audience, then when you begin writing you will push the words across the sheet.
2. If you are right-handed, you will stand to the side and somewhat "hug"

the easel stand, while keeping your left foot pointed to the audience. Then you can write and speak at the same time.
3. The pointing of the foot is what is crucial for both. It keeps your body open to the audience.
4. This takes a lot of practice to seamlessly use this tactic. Be sure to practice it before you utilize with an audience.

Technology

A person knows they are aged, possibly long in the tooth, in a particular profession, when they can reflect on their journey and see the evolution of technology within that particular profession. I am definitely in that camp.

Even if I think back to my days elementary and middle school, my teachers would use what was referred to as "overheads." The devices had a big base that would sit on a cart and had a long neck with a mirror above it. The base contained a huge light that projected a bright light upon the pull-down screen. The teacher would then have to use clear sheets with Vis-à-vis markers that were quasi-permanent to write or draw a consistent image or message for the entire class to see. This was the evolution in teaching just beyond chalk boards.

When I think about my time as a professional facilitator and presenter, I've seen the evolution from utilizing only easel sheets coupled with PowerPoints that were projected from a projector that had to sit on a desk. The projector on a desk or cabinet was interesting because cords had to be run across the floor, thusly creating a tripping hazard. It was more evident when I had to pull in a table to place it in the middle of the room to increase the size of the projected image for larger classes. This was a session that could only be delivered to those in the room with you.

Now technology has advanced, and companies are investing more in technology, that almost any trainer/presenter can be located in a room, but can reach thousands with one session. There is technology where a push of a button can lower the blinds in the room, hide the projector screen, the projector is hard wired while hanging from the ceiling, and cameras are placed in the room so the session can be broadcasted to audience members wherever they are in the world.

Even though technology has advanced, facilitators and presenters are usually on the forefront of knowing how the technology operates because it effects their sessions.

Part of the technology advancement goes beyond just the technology we use during a session. Now facilitators/presenters are being asked to train on new platforms that are needed for their audiences to succeed.

The sophistication of knowledge only continues to grow for facilitators and presenters.

This evolution is important yet the principles behind delivering a successful session remain consistent.

First and foremost, if you are delivering a session in a new space/room that has technology you haven't utilized before, part of your preparation should include getting a "walk through" of how the technology works. This means you may need to arrive earlier, either the day before or earlier in the day, to get an education on the system. I have reached out to those that have delivered sessions in that room before and scheduled time, or I've even gone so far as to schedule time with the local IT person. Either way, you want to ensure you understand at least the basics on how the system operates before your session starts.

Secondly, when you are in a position to need to demonstrate a new technology or software, you will want to get time with the technology. This may need to occur a few weeks in advance, unless you have previous experience with it.

If you are only presenting the elements of the new software (e.g. sales demo), your time and knowledge of the technology or software may not be as robust. This could be due to the software being in early phases of the release. Yet, when actually training a class on the new software, it behooves you as a trainer to have a more intimate knowledge. Trainers that have been on my teams throughout the years, along with myself, have shared a perspective that trainers need to be one of the groups that have the earliest exposure to the new technology or software.

The purpose behind getting trainers more exposure to the new technology or software is, even though it is new, the class will look at the trainer as the expert, even if it is new to everyone. The opportunity to gain an understanding of the technology or software will enhance the learning experience, thusly positively impacting the adoption rate for the class.

When Microsoft Teams was first developed and hitting the market, I was at a company that was integrating MS Teams as a productivity enhancement tool. If you are unfamiliar with MS Teams, it is essentially a one size fits all platform. There are chat features, teams channel functions, along with video call capabilities. Not to mention the ability to share documents much easier. During this integration, we were asked to move away from Webex to MS Teams as our primary virtual facilitation platform. I mention this because this is a great example of the difference between a presenter and a trainer of a new technology or software.

I, along with one of the managers on the team, were able to meet directly with representatives from Microsoft. We were meeting with them to find out if the virtual experience would be similar, if not better than Webex. During the meeting, the account rep did most of the presentation. Primarily discussing the value of the tool, along with the features and benefits, but when we started asking questions around functionality, he handed the reins over to one of their technical trainers that was able to demo the platform and speak from a position of expertise that aligned with what we needed as learning professionals. This allowed us as the audience to better understand the intricacies of the platform from a training perspective.

That point of this is depending on what the ask is of you as a facilitator or presenter, the earlier you are able to get exposure, you will set yourself up for success when it becomes your turn to deliver your session. Your audience will thank you for it.

Lastly, when you are preparing for an actual session on a new technology or software, create a navigation plan. Taking the time to prepare how you want to navigate demonstrations will maintain the seamless experience you strive to achieve.

A navigation plan is the idea to know how you are going to maneuver from your visuals (e.g. PowerPoint) to an actual system demonstration. When we dive into Audience Experience and review the Activity Cycle, we will review the importance of demos, but for now a demonstration can help an audience begin to visualize how the technology or software should function. This is an enhancement beyond just showing screenshots on a PowerPoint.

Here are elements for a successful navigation plan:

- Have all systems open
- Log into all applicable systems
- Minimize computer desktop clutter
- Close everything not needed for session (e.g. email & instant message)
- If using internet browser, only open what is needed; place browser windows/tabs in order you need them
- If screen sharing, share only the window you need

When you read through that list, it may seem like they are quite basic, yet far too often I see folks to this day still having very busy computer desktops and they get lost trying to locate the one window they need. To make it more awkward, they are doing it after they already started sharing their screen. That means all of us get to experience the navigational chaos.

There are two elements above that I want to reinforce, close everything not needed and screen sharing only what you need.

These somewhat go hand and hand and can lead to embarrassing moments and credibility reduction.

By closing everything you don't need, you can avoid awkward/embarrassing situations. There was one situation when a peer of mine got really embarrassed in front of our boss during a business review presentation. The team that I was a part of was an amazing team, I thought the world of my peers, still do. During this time, we were tasked as a leadership team to build a newly formed centralized learning organization.

One of our new practices is we would meet regularly with our boss to review the state of our teams (e.g. personnel and team performance). At one of our earlier meetings, my peer was in the middle of presenting her team's performance and she was projecting her screen through a projector onto a screen so the entire team could see it.

There was a lot of pressure during these presentations because our boss was a tough guy. His approach was a very hard approach.

We all learned a lot from him and we had to thicken our proverbial skin. Needless to say, we didn't want to make any mistakes otherwise we could be the "proud" recipient of verbal canon fire. Unfortunately, during my peers presentation, she didn't close her email and in the middle of her presentation, she got an email from a co-worker outside our team, and the preview window displayed the subject of the email and what everyone saw was, "After a long hard night of drinking..."

You could have heard a pin drop. The next words that were uttered was from our boss, "What the fuck is that?!?" Thankfully, what we assumed would occur next was a humorous exchange, but my heart immediately sank for her because you could see the embarrassment in her face.

The moral of the story: close the windows/applications you don't need.

This also connects with the concept of only screen share the window/application you need. With virtual meetings and presentation platforms (e.g. Zoom), it is easier to only share specific applications or windows. By doing this, it can prevent the situation above when in a virtual space. What is also does is it can maintain professional credibility for you as the presenter. The best example of this is when you are sharing PowerPoint slides.

It has become quite the pet peeve of mine, when I see someone presenting content from PowerPoint and it is not in presentation mode. The window being shared is the actual PowerPoint window. Which means the audience sees the raw information and the list of slides along with left hand side of the screen. By doing this, it can make it harder for the audience to read the slides and it also portrays less than professional and lazy image of the presenter.

If you want to be viewed as a professional in every circumstance, take the extra couple moments to go into presentation mode in PowerPoint, even if you are just presenting during a meeting. Your credibility will thank you.

What Preparation Does for You

Preparation are actionable tools that you can utilize to drive a higher level of confidence. The best part about it is your preparation and the steps you take to set the "stage" for your session are within your control. You can choose to complete everything you need in order to prepare or you can choose to "wing it." If I were a betting man, I would place my money on the prepared facilitator/presenter 100% of the time to deliver a great session, regardless of personality.

When you go into a session, you want to be confident and the fact that a large portion of your confidence comes your ability to prepare, lets you know the importance of filling your toolbox full of tools.

Because if you are not prepared, your audience will know. They will see it in your mannerisms and how you carry yourself.

It alleviates the "need" to read from a script. If you don't know your material, you will become dependent on your guide/notes/script and you will find yourself reading directly from the page. Adults are not toddlers. Toddlers love to be read to. Adults do not.

The biggest indicator that I've seen when a facilitator was not prepared, occurred in the first five minutes of the session. In this particular situation, I noticed some nervous mannerisms (e.g. minimal eye contact, creating barriers), and I assumed it was at the start of the session and the facilitator would flip the switch. Well...that didn't quite happen. This particular facilitator was not exuding confidence and hadn't prepared, that when he started speaking, he read his bio directly from the piece of paper he had with him. Read his own bio. One would think that we know ourselves well enough that we wouldn't need to read our bio to another human, let alone an entire audience.

Room Setup

Don't work for the room, make the room work for you.

This is advice I have given to the many presenters and facilitators I have worked with throughout my career. The room in which you are delivering your session in can be a valuable asset. If done correctly, it can enhance the experience for your audience, keep things fresh for you, and bolster the impact of your session.

There have been too many instances when I've observed facilitators/presenters and it was obvious the layout of the room was restricting them. The restrictions have been table locations, chairs in disarray, dry erase boards cluttered from a previous session, old easel sheets on the wall from different content.

This is also another reason why arriving early is so imperative because it allows you to set the room up that best fits your session.

Now you are likely asking, but what if I am unable to move anything in the room?

This is a valid and common question. There will be instances when you are presenting from a stage, there aren't any major adjustments you can make. You can't ask for the stage to be redesigned. The same thing applies to facilitators if you are training a lab room that has computers hard wired through the tables. Those situations can and will surface.

As you continue to through this section, you will gain some ideas that even minor changes (e.g. placement of your water on stage or easel placement in a lab setting) can have a positive effect on your session.

Optimal Room Set Up Tips

Assess the tables, reposition as needed.

There are many different ways to set up the tables in the room that compliments the outcomes you are striving to achieve with your session:

Rows

- By setting the tables into rows, this positions the audience to all be facing you, which aids in your ability to assess your audience. Gauging engagement through simple eye contact.
- It is much more of a traditional school set up.
- This set up also allows you the ability, especially if the class is using computers, where you can stand at the back of the room while guiding them and you have easy visibility to what is on their screens.
- The downside to utilizing rows is it makes it much harder to move throughout the room, especially if you need provide personal attention to someone in the middle of a row.
- Another downside is it is harder to make a personal connection with audience members due the lack of proximity and barriers.

Pods

- Having the tables in pods is amazing for group work and collaboration.
- If your session involves group work in the designed activities, this places the audience in the position to easily make eye contact with each other in a small group setting.
- This can be a fun set up for you because the flexibility this offers for you to move throughout the room is almost limitless. Moving around the outside of the tables, weaving throughout the pods, and delivering from the front/back/sides.
- Utilizing pods also allows for heightened connection with the audience

- because you are able to connect with the audience through proximity and minimal barriers.
- The downside to pods is it can be harder for some audience members to see you depending on where you move. If you move to the left side of the room, there could be about half the class that has to turn 180-degrees in their chairs to see you.
- Also, by having the pods set up, there is an increased ability for the audience to have side conversations with more people because they are facing each other. Depending on the class dynamics, it may require more room management from you.

U-Shape

- This has also been referred to as the "bull ring" because as the presenter/facilitator, you are able to move into the center of the group and the tables are a barrier between you and the audience, which is like watching a bull pace around a pen.
- The U-shape set up has been one of my favorites when delivering sessions. It allowed me the opportunity to engage with my audiences by adding closer proximity, yet because of the table barrier it created an additional "safety" mindset for the learners. Being a taller person, it can be less intimidating for my audiences if they have the slight barrier as I move closer to them.
- Due to the open space in the middle, if someone has a question that requires a closer connection, you are able to move closer to that person and offer assistance from the other side of the table. Plus, you don't have to attempt to navigate around chairs and others.
- A downside to the U-shape, although a value for me at times, creates a consistent barrier between you and the audience.
- In this setup, if done correctly, you will be walking backwards often. This is due to need to remain facing the audience as often as possible. Many facilitators/presenters in other cultures have mentioned to never turn our back to the audience, which has value to remain focused on the audience

and this set up forces a higher frequency of backward movement for you.

Organize the Room

First impressions are powerful, and not only do you want to make a good first impression, but your room should as well. Ensuring your room has a level of uniformity creates the impression of the type of session they are attending.

If your audience walks in and things within the room are in disarray, they will assume the session will be disorganized and unstructured.

If your audience walks in and things are organized, they will assume the session will be organized and professional.

Many of your audience may not realize they are making that snap decision, but they will.

This is why popular business icons (e.g. Andy Frisella) have mentioned that when they are interviewing candidates, they will walk with the candidate back to their car. They do this because they are finding out if the candidates actions match the words from their interview. For instance, if the candidate mentions they are organized and have attention to detail, yet their car looks like the dumpster behind a McDonald's, it is an indicator that their words don't match their actions.

The same applies with presenters and facilitators. Focusing on the details will only amplify your ability deliver the type of experience for your audience.

Those details start with your room.

I want to share the practices I have utilized in every session I've delivered to help create a level of awareness for you on the type of details in which to pay close attention. Be advised, as you read through these, you may question my sanity and even label me as obsessive. Which is fine. I want to reiterate that when I approach a session, I want to ensure I address 100% of the things that are within my control to deliver an exceptional experience for my audiences.

If you are delivering a session in a room that has computers, you will want to go through each station and place the keyboards and the corresponding mouse in the same location at each station.

Depending on the room design, I usually will push the keyboards as close to the monitor as possible, then have the mouse aligned next to the keyboard on the right. This even includes arranging the cords to be as minimally visible as possible. While you align the keyboard and mouse at each station, make sure the monitors are straight. I have gone so far to ensure all of the monitors are the same height.

Part of my process to organize the room is to strategically place my easel(s) throughout the room. Similar to what was highlighted earlier in the materials section, but when it comes to organizing the room, there are additional factors to consider.

Not only do I want to have the easel(s) placed where it adds value to the actual content, but I also take into consideration the audience traffic patterns. For instance, I may want an easel at the side of the room, but if the room size and number of tables there is only three feet between the wall and tables, placing an easel in the middle of that before the session starts, does not make for conducive walking space for the learners coming in.

This is when other options will need to be utilized for easel placement (front, back, or different side).

If things get really cramped, I have removed easels completely and hung the easel sheets on the walls. Or, I have gone so far to place the easel just outside the room, where I can easily get to it, then when the time comes, I will bring it in when it is needed.

Taking the room set up a little further, there may be instances where you need to track down some cleaning supplies to wipe down tables and/or chairs. That's right, you may need to apply some good ole fashioned "elbow grease." Too many times I've walked into a room and there was trash on the ground, random drawings on dry erase boards, or spill stains on tables, and there was no way I was going to have my audience walk into the same environment I encountered.

I have heard from presenters and facilitators before, "we have cleaning people," or "that's not my job." Both of those may be true.

But, are the cleaning people on call at 6:30/7:00 in the morning when you're preparing for an 8:00 class start time? Probably not.

Isn't it your job to create an exceptional experience for your audience? It is almost impossible to deliver an exceptional experience when the room looks messy.

It is a matter of pride and commitment that you have for your craft as a presenter or facilitator that you'll focus on the details to enhance your audience's experience. Keep in mind, this is not to say that you need to become a full-time custodial engineer and clean the entire room top to bottom. Make the room look presentable. Something you would be proud to have an audience walk into.

The details of setting up your room includes chairs. The simple focus of ensuring all the chairs are pushed into their respective spots at the tables adds to the environment you create.

If you want to take it a step further, which at this point shouldn't surprise you about me, if there are 15 people joining the session, I will try to make sure there are exactly 15 chairs available. I have taken the time in my room set up where I will move chairs out of the room and relocate them to another room, or even just outside the room. This will open up the room for easier movement and it will provide the right amount of seats for the audience which alleviates the audience from being too spread out from one another.

Then to take it one step further, if the chairs are adjustable, especially up and down, I have taken the time to ensure all the chairs are set at the exact same height.

One additional note around chairs comes from a best practice I observed early in my career. I was observing a master level trainer on a program and he set the expectation at the beginning of his session that when anyone gets up to leave, they need to push their chair in. He would even reiterate the phrase "push your chair in" even when sending them to break.

At first I thought it was odd, but after talking to the trainer afterwards, he mentioned he likes to do that because it is a basic reminder of session expectations and it maintains a level of order in the room to ensure everyone, including himself, can navigate the room easier. I've kept that tool in my toolbox going on 18 years.

There have been two different people throughout my career in which I have co-delivered a session that when I began deploying this next tip, they had the same look on their faces. It was the face that most can relate to, it was the "are you shitting me?" look.

In these two different classes, at two different times, and in two different locations, I pulled my "material uniformity" tool out of my toolbox.

This tactic takes the room set up to completely different level, at least in the eyes of other presenter/facilitators in which I've worked.

The material uniformity is focused on the audience and part of their first impression upon entering the room.

Every session that is trained will have different materials that get distributed for a session. It ultimately depends on the design of the content. What doesn't change is how they are set up.

Most of the time when you're training a class, there is a guide of some kind, that guide should be centered with the chair, which as we have already done is fully pushed into a location at a table. When presenting in an auditorium setting where tables are not present, if there is a handout, those can be placed following the lines of the chair while centered on the seat.

In most instances, when I place a guide at each spot, I will have a two to three finger width of distance between the edge of the table and the bottom of the guide.

It is good practice to offer a writing utensil (e.g. pen) for each audience member. This commonly won't be the situation for presentations without tables as the pens can easily roll of chairs, and if it is part of a larger event, the audience will receive "goody" bags filled with sponsor tchotchkes.

When I've placed a pen, there are two locations I usually place them, either along the spine of the guide or diagonally centered at the top of the guide.

Both options maintain the level of uniformity and it is not covering up the title page of the guide.

One of the best things I have leaned on throughout my career and I am always so happy to have them present in the room for a session are name tents.

I love these because with all of the things I am constantly trying to remember during a session, it takes a little while to remember names. These name tents are amazing, and I glance at them often during a session so I can ensure I am addressing each audience member by name. Which is great for bolstering credibility and engagement.

If you have not used them before, name tents are the heavier weight paper that are smaller than a regular sheet of paper (8.5x11) and are folded in half. Audience members are able to write their name on them and place them at their spot, almost like a reservation card.

When I am setting up each spot for a session, the name tents will go directly above where the guide is placed on the table, usually about 3-5 fingers of separation.

The last few examples have leaned more toward the facilitation side of things with the additional supplies that may not be necessary for a presentation, the next two are important for both facilitators and presenters.

Understanding the layout of the room as it pertains to the projector light is important. As previously mentioned in movement, to avoid those unfortunate circumstances of walking through the projector light with less than preferred graphics on your person, you will need to know where in the room you can move to avoid the projector light.

I utilize something that is very common in theatre, which is the using "marks" for certain placement. In full disclosure, I did not grow up acting on stage nor am I trained in all of the terminology so my terminology may be off.

If you have ever been on a stage where a play is held, if you look at the ground there are many different marks all over the floor of the stage. These are what I will call "marks." These are designated spots that performers need to get to at different parts of the play. This is to help ensure the correct lighting is available, not obstructing background exchanges, or being in the right spot for their next interaction with another cast member. They are subtle points that are unseen by the audience.

The same applies when presenting or facilitating. I have had to utilize certain "marks" on the floor of the room I am delivering a session in to know where I can walk to avoid walking through a projector light. I have counted carpet tiles away from the front wall or even placed a small piece of blue painters' tape on the floor as an indicator. The painters' tape is helpful as it can be pulled up easily and doesn't place you on the Building Supervisor's "Naughty List."

There will be instances where the projector is lower (e.g. on a table or stand) and there is no way to walk beneath the light. There was an instance when I was observing a session in Enid, Oklahoma and the building was an old department store. This particular training room was long and the trainer's desk was at the front of the room and the projector was on the table casting the light across the only "exit" point from behind the trainers desk. As I was observing the session, the trainer remained at the front of the room the entire time because they had been taught not to walk through the projector light. They felt trapped. The only movement they felt they could do was in a 3'x3' section behind the desk.

What the trainer forgot about was another powerful tool at our disposal when training or presenting from PowerPoint slides. It is the magic of the "blackout" button on slide advancers.

Most, if not all, slide advancers have a button that will blank the screen. This turns the screen black. I am a fan of this functionality because it can change the focus of the audience, which can alleviate over visual stimulation. It also provides a very subtle way to aid presenters and facilitators to move seamlessly throughout the room without needing to walk through the projector light. If you are not familiar with this function on your slide advancer, I'd recommend finding it and knowing where it is on your device. If by chance, you don't have one, the "B" key on your keyboard will do the exact same thing when your slides are in presentation mode.

The last tip on room set-up is having your guide or notes in an optimal location. It would wonderful if there was one single spot that I could recommend to "place it here." However, every room I've delivered sessions ranging between old bank vaults in basements with an audience of seven to venues with a large stage with an audience of hundreds. Each situation called for identifying the most ideal spot for my notes or guide to be placed.

The intent with finding your ideal location is to have them located somewhere that is easy for you to get to and where you can remain visible, almost like a "home base."

If you place your notes/guide in the far back corner of the room behind the audience when you are primarily delivering your session at the front, that is likely not an ideal location. You want to have your notes or guide in a spot where you can plan your movement to maintain the seamless experience for your audience.

Let's say for instance you're like me, and you have pages that you will be utilizing throughout your session and you carry 1-2 pages with you as you move through the room. As you get to the last portion of the last page, you want your guide in a spot that as you are covering your last few points you are working your way toward your "home base." This puts you in a position that by the time you get to your "home base" you are ready to exchange your 1-2 pages for the next 1-2 pages. This also prevents you from needing to carry a clunky binder around the room with you.

Also, by having a "home base" and only taking a few pages with you at a time, you won't run into that awkward situation when you get caught up in the moment and you set your guide/notes down to demonstrate something for your audience (e.g brainstorm on a dry erase board). This leads to continuing your thought and engagement with the audience and before you know it, you are somewhere else in the room and you want to refer to your notes, then you realize, you forgot where you placed them. By no means is this the end of the world, but it can be embarrassing when you end up having to ask the audience, "where did I place my notes?" And yes, I have done that before.

Preparation Sequence

The level of detail that it takes to deliver an exceptional experience is something that many who have not truly learned about presenting and facilitating never realize. As you've seen thus far, if you are committed to creating an exceptional experience, there are many minute details that can easily be overlooked.

This always frustrated me if I forgot to prepare something before a session and didn't realize I missed something until I needed it, or it was too late to do something about. Through the number of sessions I've delivered throughout my career, I realized that I needed to create a default setting for myself when it came to preparing. There should be items that would be second nature and I wouldn't have to invest a lot of additional brain power to remember everything. Then I could focus on the unique preparation steps that arise for each session (e.g. easel sheet preparation).

Through years of refinement, this is why I utilize a Preparation Sequence.

The Preparation Sequence is a series of tasks, possibly rituals, that I do every time I prepare for a session. This concept came about when I sat back to reflect on how I was preparing and what I realized, I was doing the same tasks/rituals. Every. Single. Time.

When I came to this realization, I wrote out the common components and the epiphany I had was I had done them for so long, they just became 2nd nature. Any time I had a session to deliver, these things were occurring without any additional planning or thought.

If you have facilitated classes or presented on a stage, you have likely heard the concept of a preparation checklist. These are very helpful, and I have used these. For me, the checklists were very targeted to the specific session I was delivering (i.e. easel prep, testing projectors, etc.).

The Preparation Sequence were habits that are refined and programmed into your brain that your brain and body know that once you flip that switch to move toward delivering an exceptional experience, the habits built and refined start at the time in which you've programmed them. This has become so valuable for me because as a presenter/facilitator, there are so many things that run through my brain and I am trying to remember (e.g. key talking points), that if I can optimally get prepared without thinking about it, I have found it reduces my mental fatigue.

Each person may have a sequence that is unique to them and may not work exactly for someone else, which is ok. We are all unique.

I will walk through my Preparation Sequence. Some of the items will look familiar from earlier portions of this book and some may be familiar to you as things you do to get prepared. Just remember, this is the process I use and when you craft yours, it may be similar, it may vastly different, but the goal is to save your brain power for your session.

Be prepared, when you look at the 24 habits I have built as part of my Preparation Sequence, obsessed is a word that may run through your head, but at this point, it shouldn't surprise you. In addition, many of the items can be captured on a checklist, but these are the habits, that no matter what, are done before one of my sessions.

Dean's Preparation Sequence

Days leading up to the session:

1) See the room for the session.

- As mentioned previously, I need to see the room before I walk in the day of the event. Many times, this occurs the day before, but I have had folks take a picture and send it to me.

2) Visualize plan for session.

- After seeing the room, I begin thinking through how I want the room to be set-up. I also start strategizing how and where I can move throughout the room, especially to engage the audience.

3) Make appropriate highlights in notes/guides.

- If these have not been completed previously (e.g. new session), I utilize my highlighter strategy to align my thoughts. If it is a training session and opportunity presents itself to observe the session before I deliver it, this is usually when I will complete my highlights. (Note, based on schedules, this observation may occur weeks in advance.

4) Ensure appropriate supplies are available.

- Depending on the session being delivered, I coordinate to have the supplies with me and/or if larger supplies are needed (e.g. easels) obtain confirmation they will be onsite the day before.

5) Ensure materials are available.

- This one usually occurs simultaneously with the last one. If there are items needed for the audience, ensure printing is completed and shipping has them arriving no later than 1-2 day prior. Side note, if I am shipping the materials, I always make sure I know who is receiving them and I connect with them early so I know exactly where they will be at when I arrive.

PREPARATION

Night before session:

6) Review notes.

- This habit is one I was taught very early in my career, and it made so much sense for me because I hadn't considered it. Whether it is the first time or hundredth time I've delivered the session, I want to make sure I am priming my brain to focus on the specific content for the next day.

7) Review roster.

- There have been situations when I may not have visibility to the roster of audience members before a session. If a roster is available, I like to review the names of attendees. I look for multiples of the same name (e.g. three people with the first name of Jack) or if someone's name is a longer version of a common name, I make a mental note that I will want to obtain clarity on the preferred name.

  For instance, if a name is showing as "Alexander," I want to make a mental note to clarify if they prefer "Alexander" or "Alex." In the situations of presenting to a larger audience, I will review any available demographics. Knowing the make-up of the audience helps to prime my brain. This is especially important if stories or examples are utilized because it helps ensure the stories or examples are applicable to the audience.

8) Revisit mental room set up.

- Since I have a mental picture in my head of the room, I revisit my preliminary strategy for how I want to use the room effectively.

9) Eat protein heavy dinner.

- I focus on a heavier protein meal the night before because depending on the start time of the session, I may not get an opportunity to eat before starting a session. The heavier dose of protein helps ensure I don't wake up feeling hungry and have the energy to sustain into the session.

Day of Session:

10) Drink water.

- As soon as I wake up, I drink a large amount of water, usually 30oz. This rehydrates me after sleeping overnight. It also starts me down the path to ensure I don't get too thirsty throughout the session.

11) Exercise.

- I don't get too crazy with this exercise session, but I need to get my body moving first thing in the morning. It helps to prime my body for being "on" during the session. If I am traveling, I will usually go down to the hotel fitness center and simply walk on the treadmill. If the fitness center is busy or non-existent, I will walk around the outside of the hotel. Just for fun, I will usually add in 100 push-ups in the morning, after I've had a chance to move a little bit.

12) Stretch.

- After getting some movement, I like to stretch. This has been helpful for me because I can continue to keep my body loose, especially after getting some exercise. It also helps to alleviate tightness during the session.

13) Shower.

- This may seem like a no-brainer because let's be honest, we don't want to stink while we are trying to engage our audience. Still part of the routine. The one element that may be unique is I take a regular warm shower, but before I get out of the shower, I will lower the temperature of the shower. I make it as cold as I can tolerate. This helps me wake up even more. It is around this time when my body is reminded, it is "go" time.

14) Watch a comedy show or stand-up.

- This was much harder to get my exact show to watch until YouTube exploded and now anything can be found there. It is much easier for me to get a show I want to watch now than before when I had to ensure I had a portable DVD player and haul DVDs with me. If I watch a stand-up, it's either Tim Allen or John Pinnette, and if I watch a sit-com, its either Big Bang Theory or Rules of Engagement. My selection ultimately depends on the mood and the session I'm delivering that day. Any of these options run for ~20-25 minutes.

15) Sing.

- This is a bit more of my quirky element, but when commuting to the location for the session (from hotel or home), I have certain songs that I listen to on the way. While commuting I will sing in the car. The vocal warm-up primes my vocal cords for the day. The three songs I will sing on the way are "Love Will Keep Us Alive" by the Eagles, "A Wink and A Smile" by Harry Connick Jr, and "For the First Time" by Darius Rucker. Others may get added depending on the commute time.

16) Caffeinate.

- My morning staple is a 5-shot Iced Americano from Starbucks. I will also have at least one small cup of hot, black coffee. The warm drink helps open my voice and the Americano is what I sip on throughout the morning. I also will keep an energy drink on hand for later in the day/session. My go-tos are Celsius or a 1st Phorm energy drink.

17) Set up room.

- Once I arrive at the location for the session, and I walk in the door for the room I'm in, I begin getting things set up to match what I'd visualized leading into the day. If tables need to be moved, trash picked up, chairs pushed in, etc.

18) Listen to Training Prep playlist.

- That's right, more music. I have a specific playlist that I listen to in order once I am in set up mode. This allows me to really start building my energy level in preparation for the session. Without a doubt, the first three songs I play on the playlist are "Toast" by Heywood Banks, "Rubberband Man" by The Spinners, and "Low Rider" by War. And that is the exact order in which I listen to them.

19) Appropriately place materials, if applicable.

- If there are materials for the audience that need to be set up, I will do this while listening to my Training Prep playlist.

20) Set up computer, test media.

- I will also set up my computer early to make sure everything is working so in the event it doesn't I have time to remedy.

21) Set up additional supplies.

- This particular step in the sequence is dependent upon whether there are additional supplies to set up (e.g. Easel sheets). The timing of this for me is now it is thinking more about the content and the experience as it is now closer to "show time."

22) Find isolated area for big movements.

- Depending on the location of the room for my session, I may need to find an isolated spot close by that I can step into for some big movements. The movements have included hopping in place, power posing, some additional stretches. These will depend on how my body is feeling and what parts need to be activated.

23) Send Buddy Text.

- This is something I incorporated after having an opportunity to deliver a number of sessions with one of my former colleagues and a good friend, Samantha Schwartz. Before any session I deliver, I send her a very specific, yet silly text. It is the same quick text each time. We do it for each other and we know as soon as that text comes in, we know the other one is about to deliver a session. I won't share exactly what it is we text, but it has become part of my routine. This can be important because even though our exchange is silly in nature, it never hurts to be reminded going into a session, that you are supported, and someone believes in you.

24) Engage audience members, if applicable

- Last but not least, if it is a more intimate setting, I will greet the audience members as they arrive. Keep in mind, this may start while you are setting up the room because there are people that like to arrive to a session 45 minutes early.

The Preparation Sequence is something I have used to create the proverbial "muscle memory" so when I am getting ready to deliver a session, I have less to think about because I have programmed my mind and body to operate a certain way so I can deliver my best possible session.

Your Preparation Sequence will look different from mine. The key is to identify the steps you need to take to ensure you are optimized and after enacting the sequence long enough, it will become a habit that you don't have to think about it anymore or you won't need to ensure those particular steps are captured on a checklist.

8

AUDIENCE EXPERIENCE

Ensuring your audience has an exceptional experience should be your #1 priority. There is value in ensuring the goals or objectives for your session are achieved. However, I have seen too often an over-dependency of focusing solely on the goals or objectives of a session. That creates a "check-the-box" activity.

A "check-the-box" activity is the situation where we can state something was completed. Did the audience achieve the desired score? Was the audience able to demonstrate a particular skill?

Only focusing on the goals or objectives of a session leaves an audience with the feeling that when asked about the session, their response would likely be, "I learned something, but it was ok."

Your goal as a presenter or facilitator should be that when your audience leaves your session, they have reactions similar to, "that was an awesome class, and I actually learned something."

Focus on the Experience

In order to create an exceptional audience experience, the focus on the experience needs to be your top priority. If people enjoy the experience, I have found that they are more receptive to learning new ideas and applying those ideas to become better than they were before they walked in.

If your audience is open to new ideas or ways of being better, then your success rate of achieving the goals or objectives of a session will go up.

At one of the previous companies I worked, I was invited to attend a series of leadership meetings for a particular business group I was providing learning support for. One portion of the agenda, they invited an outside speaker to come in and his focus was on helping this room full of leaders to enhance their presentation skills. Being a competitive person, I was immediately skeptical as I had already been delivering sessions for over 16 years at this point. However, my rational brain kicked in and I figured, that based on his bio, I bet there is something I could learn from this gentleman.

About 30 minutes into his four-hour session, this was a "check-the-box" activity for this presenter. He was slated to deliver a prescribed list of topics and conduct a certain amount of activities. Don't get me wrong, from working with this group, I knew it was a tough crowd, however, I knew they were all willing to learn and grow. I don't want to disparage another person that is putting themselves out there by leading a session, but if I had to guess, if he were to self-assess his session, he would likely say it wasn't his best effort.

Throughout the session, he delivered very basic concepts and the activities that were completed didn't gauge learning application. It also didn't appear that he took the time to understand the dynamics of the audience because there were times he was speaking to this room full of upper level leaders as if they were beneath him. To make matters worse, at the end of his time, he asked if there any questions, and I couldn't believe the last words he said, which I remember vividly, "Well I can see everyone is not listening so I will wrap up for the day."

WHAT?!?!?

That was the last impression this guy left with his audience. I couldn't believe it.

This particular gentleman hadn't connected with the audience and wasn't focused on creating an exceptional audience experience that by the end of the time, he'd lost the group.

Part of focusing on the audience experience ties directly back to the duck on the pond analogy. Your audience should see you floating along as if nothing can bother you. That seamless experience starts with the mindset that everything that plays out is intentional, even if it's an accident.

I have handled one of the most common "accidents" during a session, technology not working, a couple different ways which I mentioned earlier: casually refer to the situation with a humorous quip ("I guess the internet gremlins didn't like the next slide") then try quickly to get the slides back or I will send them on an impromptu break ("this brings us to the part of our day of what I like to call an impromptu break, how does that sound?").

Both keep it lighthearted and adds a little bit of humor. For me, cracking a joke about the situation not only prevents stress from spreading from me to the audience, but it helps keep my stress level minimized.

These situations can be stressful, and most of the time, they are not caused by you as the facilitator or presenter, so there is no need to apologize to the audience. Apologizing to the audience places you in the role of culprit for the situation. You don't have control of the slides not working. You don't have control if the projector stops working. Not apologizing to the audience is VERY HARD. It is a default process for most because we feel bad that the experience has been impacted, especially because we've invested so much time into creating an exceptional experience.

Avoid Narrating Your Actions

To maintain a focus on the experience for your audience, approach your session like you are having a conversation with your audience. In Authenticity, we reviewed that if you are in front of an audience and trying to be something you're not, this will not lead to a great experience. The reason I mention this, if you approach your session like a conversation, it will sound natural. Because far too often, I have seen presenters and facilitators, more so facilitators, narrate their actions.

Narrating actions always comes across as awkward. I will usually see this when a facilitator will say something like, "Let's have a discussion." This usually occurs because in the guide, it has a discussion planned as part of the content. Which is definitely a great tactic for audience engagement.

Think about the last conversation you had with your significant other or best friend, at any point did you utter the words, "let's have a discussion." I feel confident asserting you didn't.

More than likely, if you want to hear their thoughts or engage them, you will just ask a question. Right?

The same approach should be taken within your session. When it comes time to engage the audience or have them share their thoughts, ask the question. Usually there is a question that is listed in the guide or your notes to initiate the discussion. Just ask the question.

Empathy Mindset

As you are engaging with your audiences, if you haven't already, it will become apparent that everyone is different in how they learn and comprehend your message or content. This understanding that everyone will be different in how they learn (i.e. varying experiences, personal struggles, etc) will be a power tool for your toolbox of skills. The ability to demonstrate empathy will add a great deal of connection with your audiences.

There are many times you will be tested while you are in front of audiences, not necessarily because someone is being difficult, but audience members may just struggle to absorb the content you're delivering. We have all been there when learning something new. It is part of our role is to help ensure others can be brought along. Since we are so close to the subject matter that we are delivering it can be an easy trap to walk into as a presenter or facilitator to start thinking, "what is so hard about this, why don't they get it?"

There was a stretch of time when I was delivering a lot of trainer certification courses in different countries, and I had been delivering the exact same training so often, I could've delivered the content from memory. I was so immersed in the content and knew it so well, I found myself getting frustrated often on concepts that I had spoken about many times over because in my mind it wasn't that difficult. It was during a session I was delivering in Kingston, Ontario when the realization hit me.

The day before the session, the Training Manager in this particular location made a passive comment that was the epiphany I needed. In conversation focused on preparation for the next day, she mentioned, "the group is excited for the class tomorrow, but they are nervous since they haven't had a training like this." I bet if I were to ask her today if she recalls the conversation, she likely wouldn't, but it was the reality check I needed at that time. I had forgotten that individuals are new to the content I was training. It was the mindset shift I needed and I still refer back to periodically in those times when I begin to get outside of the audience empathy mindset. What may not be new to you, is likely brand new to someone else.

Keeping the empathy mindset at the ready when you are delivering your session will aid in your ability to understand your audience. This can be even more valuable on a daily basis if your session runs over a couple days. An engaged learner one day, can come in the next and be completely disengaged. Perhaps they were up all night with a sick child. Perhaps their power went out that morning. Perhaps they got into a car accident after the previous days session. Circumstances can change. Life can happen. It is our ability to understand and place ourselves in the shoes of audience members will drive tremendous engagement from your audience.

Demonstrating empathy toward your audience with the understanding that each person entering your session is unique will position you for a great connection with them as individuals. There is another side of that coin and that is understanding their professional life.

Understand Their Business.

Understanding the audience's business is like having an impact wrench in your toolbox. If you are not familiar with an impact wrench, this is tool that is most common at tire dealers. When you get new tires on your vehicle, or possibly getting a tire repaired, as you are walking into the building, you inevitably hear an impact wrench. It is the loud tool that when it is not trying to remove a lug nut from a tire, and you pull the trigger it makes somewhat of a whizzing sound. It is powered by being connected to an air compressor, yet it doesn't look like a classic wrench you may have at home, it looks more like a drill, trigger and all. The really cool thing about an impact wrench is the force that powers the wrench.

The value of an impact wrench is if you've ever had to change a tire without an impact wrench, you know that trying to get lug nuts off a tire with anything else can be very tough.

As we think about why this is important. We know that with the various audience members that enter our sessions, some are amiable to what we are delivering and there are others that don't have a lot of interest. In most cases, it is because they feel the presenter or facilitator doesn't know their job, so how can they learn from someone that doesn't know their business.

By investing time to understand the job of those in the audience can make an impact (see what I did there?).

Don't get me wrong, it may be impossible to completely understand every facet of their job. However, it is important to ask questions going into a session to understand the type of environment the audience works within, what are their successes, and pain points. Understanding these basic elements allows you the opportunity build your credibility to connect your content to their environment.

As you learn more, as you are preparing your material, you can make notes in your presenter notes or facilitator guides as a reminder. The reference points could be the connection of how the material can positively impact their roles. This type of connection to their daily professional life is the utilization of your "impact wrench."

As your skill-set and experience grows, you will find it is easier to connect on-the-job elements to the content being delivered. You may have an understanding and how those connections are made can come through discussions during your session. Asking specific questions during your session can draw the deeper insights into their professional world and knowing the material, you will be able to articulate the value of your content on how it will improve their professional performance.

A valuable way to connect your session toward impacting your audience's roles is by connecting activities and application discussions to role expectations and on-the-job application. Any opportunity to connect those dots will drive value for the learners within your audience. Later in this section, we will dive deeper into how to effectively utilize questions to drive discussions and how to best set up activities that create will drive value for your audience.

The last few things to consider when focusing on the experience are:
   -Room Temperature
   -Material Availability
   -Sight lines
   -Awareness of potential distractions

The room temperature is often overlooked during preparations, yet it can be an element that if not managed appropriately can keep the learners from truly focusing on your session.

I had a situation when I was training a class in the Philippines. Being from Colorado, I am acclimated to a dry climate with minimal humidity. When you get to the countries, such as the Philippines, that are at sea level, there is a lot of humidity. Not only that, but the temperature stays quite a bit warmer compared to Colorado.

When I arrived at the call center to deliver the session, I was already starting to sweat. Keep in mind, we worked overnight to mirror the US business hours, so my walking commute through the mall for "breakfast" was around 7:30pm. Even in the evening hours, it was still muggy and hot for me.

As I continued to prepare the room for the session, I was sweating even more. Due to this, I dropped the temperature in the room from 75-degrees to 69-degrees. Even with that little bit of temperature difference the air conditioning kicked on, it felt wonderful.

I overlooked the first sign when learners started to arrive and immediately commented on how "cold" it was in the room. I kept it at that temperature because I thought it felt great. The session started and about an hour into the session, I noticed that every single person in the room, aside from myself, had either put on a coat, grabbed a blanket, or was rubbing their arms.

The temperature I'd set was way too frigid for my Filipino friends. I had to adjust the temperature in the room. It was the realization that it is not about what makes you comfortable as the presenter or facilitator, the audience's comfort needs to be accounted for.

This can be tough because when you are delivering a session, you are moving and your entire body is in motion so your body temperature will stay higher, yet the audience is stationary in their seats the majority of the time.

Due to this lesson, I found that there can be a compromise in how the temperature is regulated for everyone. In the example above, we ended up settling on a temperature around 72-degrees. This warmed up the audience and it wasn't too warm for me where I'd end up sweating the entire day. Trust me, a "sweaty Dean" is not a good look.

The next thing to consider is around material availability. Similar to what was mentioned in the Preparation section, any material that supports your session should be available during the session. Something else to keep in mind, there may be additional material the audience may need before or after the class. This could be simply sending the additional material via email, when it may be needed (before or after) or having a location where the audience can access it. SharePoint is a great place, especially within a company, to place additional content. You will just need to make sure the audience can access that central location.

Sight lines are commonly something that is overlooked until they become an issue. If you think back to the room set-up portion of the Preparation section,

I mentioned the adage I have repeated thousands of times throughout my career, don't work for the room, make the room work for you. Sight lines are a little more of a nuance, yet it can impact the audience experience. A large majority of the presenters and facilitators I have worked with stumble into the situation of not realizing where they are moving or where they place visuals within the room that impact the experience for their audience.

The most common sight line situation occurs when the room is set up in pods which means unless you are at the front of the room, the majority of the class will need to physically adjust how they are sitting to see you or the visuals. This is not to say that you can't place visuals throughout the room when in pods, but the experience can be enhanced if you take into account amount of effort the audience needs to shift when moving to a different area.

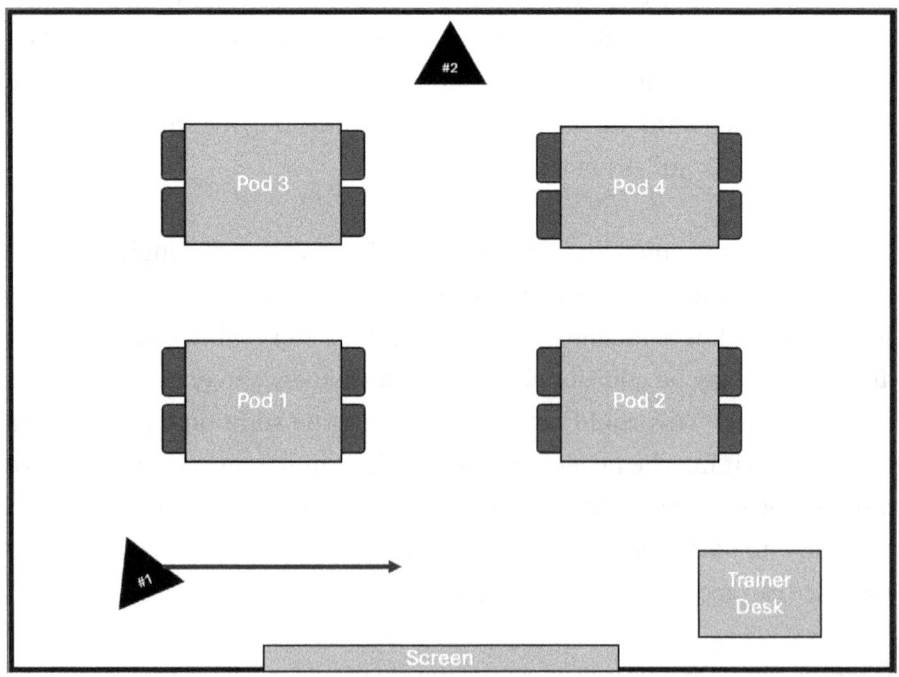

This is image is a very basic layout of for a pod style room. You can see where the better spots are for visuals when in a pod set up. The triangle (#1) is the most common placement of an easel stand. It utilizes a Diagonal Sight Line strategy for your audience. By placing your visuals in a diagonal sight line, you now will keep your audience engaged without driving too much effort for them to completely turnaround or contort their body to see you and/or your visual.

You will notice the arrow going from left to right. This is indicating that in situations where you're brainstorming a larger list of items, you can move the easel stand to the center of the room. Or, you can utilize the other triangle (#2), which would be placed in the center back of the room. This can be advantageous because it opens opportunities for you to move to another part of the room and it changes perspective for your audience.

- Side note - after seeing this example you may start to feel anxious or irritated. This is likely caused by "Yeah, but" Syndrome. You are not alone. Many come down with a case of "Yeah, but" Syndrome when examples like this are covered.

This is how it usually shows up:

- "Yeah, but my rooms are able to be set up in pods."
- "Yeah, but the rooms I use aren't that big."
- "Yeah, but I train classes in a warehouse."

It is ok if you find yourself coming down with a case of "Yeah, but" Syndrome. It happens to us all. However, the intent to is get you thinking differently and creatively about your sessions. Look for the opportunities to "make the room work for you, don't work for the room." This will help you enhance your audience experience.

The last element in which to be aware when you are focusing on the audience experience is being aware of potential distractions. Notice I didn't mention eliminate distractions. This is because there may be situations that drive distractions for a class that are completely out of our control.

Windows are the biggest culprit of distractions. This is because we cannot remove the windows, yet we need to understand what is on the other side of the window and it will be a distraction.

There was a period of time, when I was delivering a presentation skills training and the only room available was a meeting/training room. Ok, so no big deal, right? Well, two of the walls of the rooms had huge windows, one set of windows faced outside of the building and the other wall was comprised of floor to ceiling glass that faced the breakroom. Suffice to say, there was ample distractions that were going to occur throughout the session.

This is when our ability to adjust to the circumstance demonstrates your ability to keep the audience experience regardless of the situation. When life gives you lemons, you make lemonade…or lemon slices…or lemon wedges… or lemon scented potpourri. The point is your ability or adapt to keep the experience in focus is the sign that you are all in.

For the situation where the session I was delivering in essentially one big fish bowl, I decided to minimize distraction as much as possible and squeeze the most fun out of this situation. The first thing I did was to place blank easel sheets and place them evenly apart (~12-inches) along the glass wall facing the breakroom. The line of easel sheets were the same level across, with the attempt to cover the average height of most humans. The alignment was focused on keeping the room presentable and professional. It also got folks thinking we would use these eventually as part of an activity.

Most importantly it minimized the sight line distractions for the audience. Now here's where I tried to lean into having fun throughout the session. When we got to the preparation portion of the session, I walked the group through the "tiger face/lemon face" process, yet now I pivoted and instead of only me demonstrating it, I had the entire group stand up and do it with me. Any time I have had an audience do this with me, this injects significant silliness into the session. Attendees start to feel a little silly, but now that was amped up because having a room of 15 people doing "tiger face/lemon face" while standing inside of a fishbowl room made it even more fun.

I even acknowledged it when they were done. I told the group, "It is always fun to do this activity, but it is so much more fun when we do this and we get to watch the reactions of the people walking by, the reactions are priceless." In addition, if there was a larger distraction when everyone's eyes looked outside the window (e.g. a large group walking by), I would acknowledge it. Something to the effect of, "that was odd, I wonder where all those folks were going." This acknowledgement of something the obviously distracted everyone lets them know you saw it and I have found; it will help the group immediately refocus on you and your session.

The reason I mention this particular story is it is easy to get frustrated in situations that are out of our control, but as long as you maintain that laser focus on the experience for your audience, you will be surprised the level of creativity that will flood your brain.

Impactful Openings

Now that we understand the power of maintaining our focus on the experience, we need to understand effective ways to start the session.

When beginning a session, you want to get off to a strong start. To use a fishing analogy, this is when you set the hook. I am not an avid fisherman, but I have gone fishing enough and one of the lessons my uncle taught me when I was around the age of 12 was when your line is in the water and you feel a nibble, or tug, on the line, then you have to give the fishing rod a quick jerk. This sets the hook in the lip of the fish. You will know if it is set because immediately the fish will be aggressively swimming away.

An *Impactful Opening* is when you set the hook with your audience.

Have you seen the movie, Top Gun: Maverick? It was the long-awaited sequel released 2022, thirty-six years after the original (Top Gun). The movie stars Tom Cruise in both movies and he is a naval fighter pilot. Top Gun: Maverick is one of the greatest sequels, if not the greatest in movie history (in my humble opinion).

In this 2022 release, Maverick is tasked with preparing new crop of fighter pilots for a difficult mission into enemy territory. Without spoiling anything for anyone that hasn't seen the movie, leading into a pulse-pounding, adrenaline-rush ending, each of the fighter pilots have a call sign. Their mission call sign was "Dagger." That resonated with me because it was strong call sign. One might say it was **impactful**.

This impactful name is what prompted this framework for Impactful Openings: DAGR.

DAGR stands for:

- Draw Them In
- Agenda
- Goal(s)
- Review

This framework is designed to ensure it achieves the impact, or "splash," when starting a session.

Let's breakdown the framework:

Draw Them In

When starting a session, it is helpful to catch the attention of the audience to help them focus on you and the content. This can be done via:

- Story
- Quote
- Discussion
- Visuals (e.g. pictures)

Regardless of the tactic deployed, it must be relevant and can easily be connected to the content. When utilizing this tactic, it should be quick to the point. I've seen facilitators and presenters start a 60-minute session and they spend 10 minutes at the start telling a story. There is a high likelihood you will have lost the audience no later than minute TWO.

Remember: Succinct and Purposeful

Agenda

Learners, especially adult learners, like to know the path they will be taking during a session. I like to view this as a "Road Map" to the final destination. Depending on the length of the session, it will dictate the number of key points on the agenda. This doesn't have to be overly elaborate; it is ultimately an overview of the journey in which you are taking your audience toward their final destination.

The final destination being the *Goal*.

Goal

The Goal serves two purposes:

1. Value/WIIFM - what is the benefit to the audience members?
2. Objectives - what does your session want to achieve?

The WIIFM is the common acronym utilized in the learning profession that stands for What's In It For Me. Thinking back to the fishing analogy, this is the moment when you can really set the hook into your audience. If the Value or WIIFM is skipped the audience won't see how your session benefits them and can lead to disengagement.

The Objectives are the portion in which the audience sees what your content is designed to achieve.

It is possible that your Value/WIIFM are contained in the Objectives, however it is more impactful if they work in tandem.

For instance, if I were to outline the Goal during a session on Impactful Openings, it may sound something like this:

(Objectives) By the end of this session, you will be able to:

- Outline the DAGR steps, and
- Demonstrate the ability to use the DAGR method.

(Value/WIIFM) Your ability to understand DAGR steps and apply them today, you will be able to create a memorable and Impactful Opening for any session you deliver.

Then once you've caught their attention, outlined the path for your session, and established your goal, it is time to wrap up your opening.

Review

This is the simplest step. This step would only be applicable in a facilitated session as it is inviting lingering questions. When presenting, and it is pushing content, it is not designed for two-way communication. Unless there is time allocated at the end for questions regarding the subject matter.

It is simply asking the question, "What questions do you have before we begin?"

Notice the question is not, "Do you have any questions" or "Are there any questions?"

The open-ended nature of the question accomplishes two things:

1. Assumes there are questions.
2. Indirectly establishes a "give & take" protocol for the entire session.

By asking the question, it aids in focusing the attention of the audience because if someone is thinking about a question, they are likely going to be distracted by the unanswered question, instead of focusing on what you're covering.

DAGR Best Practices

Best Practice #1 - Opening <10% of total run time.

Impactful Openings, using the DAGR framework, should run no more than 10% of the total time of your session. For instance, if your session is scheduled for 60 minutes, your Impactful Opening should be no more than 6 minutes.

The reason for your opening being no longer than 10% of the total run time of your session is it keeps it focused and purposeful. It also avoids the situations of unnecessarily long stories or starting to review content, while in the opening. The most extreme case I've seen was in a trainer certification class and one of the attendees was doing a 20-minute teachback to demonstrate all they'd learned. This particular participant did not set themselves up for success as their opening ran for 10-minutes. That was 50% of the time only on the opening.

The situation was made worse by starting to review content in the opening.

Best Practice #2 - Keep agenda high level.

It is easy to slide into context setting which then leads to covering content. This usually happens when reviewing the agenda. When reviewing the agenda, keep it high level. The agenda is intended to be a teaser of what's to come.

We see this a lot in the movie industry. Before a movie comes out there will be teasers and trailers that are released to get the audience excited to the upcoming release of the movie. The same concept applies with the agenda review within an Impactful Opening.

Best Practice #3 - Preview demonstrations.

When you're in a situation of facilitating session (e.g. training a class), there is likely going to be an opportunity for the class to apply what they've learned. Previewing that the class will be placed in a situation where they will have to demonstrate their skills will add great value for your class.

When placed into a training environment, adults don't like to be surprised, especially if they are going to be in a position of demonstrating something in front of others. Whether it is a teachback or even a role play, adult learners like to know something is coming. By providing a preview of these situations, it will help them focus to ensure they will grab the information they need and can be set up for success.

In most situations, the objectives will shine a spotlight on this. Refer back to the example objectives provided in the Goal section, "Demonstrate the ability to use the DAGR method." This is what that objective is intended to highlight. Yet, one thing I have learned is being intentional with how that is reinforced is helpful.

Using the sample objective for demonstrating the DAGR method, the best practice would be to add more depth as to how they will demonstrate that. In this situation, after covering the objective, I would add, "Each person will conduct a 5-minute Impactful Opening teachback of a topic of your choice using the DAGR method. You will also receive feedback on the steps you achieved and some possible enhancement opportunities."

This will provide an appropriate preview of how they will demonstrate the skills they learned.

Best Practice #4 - Establish Ground Rules

Depending on the length of your session or the type of session, establishing ground rules for your sessions is a way to level set expectations with the audience. This practice will predominately be utilized within a facilitated session, and if done correctly, it would be possible to establish them during a presentation.

Taking the opportunity to ensure everyone that is part of the session (you & your audience) is aligned on expectations and help align on what it will take to get the most out of the session. They don't have to be overly elaborate and can be three to four items, sometimes the simpler the better.

Here are a few Ground Rules I utilize the most:

1. 100% Engagement/Participation
2. Silence cell phones/Close computers
3. "Vegas" Rules
4. Have fun!!!

Asking the audience to participate or remain engaged is setting the expectation that their involvement adds a richness to the session. Audience members will get more out of the session if everyone is involved, which includes activities, asking questions, etc.

Silencing cell phones and closing computers is strictly due to the fact when a phone goes off in the middle of the session, it can be very disruptive. Everyone immediately looks to see who's phone is chiming and it can impact the flow of the content. I also acknowledge with the audience that life outside of the session doesn't stop (work or personal) and if they need to take a call, I ask them just to kindly step out then come back when they're done. I also add in the laptop because it is very annoying when you, or someone in your session, is talking and there is a persistent clicking of keys on a keyboard.

"Vegas" Rules is a tie to the Las Vegas ad campaign, "What happens in Vegas, stays in Vegas." The same thing applies during a session, we want to create a space where audience members feel comfortable enough to share ideas or examples without fear of being chastised or ridiculed.

The last one is one of the most important to me. I want my audience to enjoy the experience. If they are enjoying the experience and having fun along the way, they will likely learn more and walk away from the experience with an exceptional experience.

When it comes to establishing Ground Rules and setting expectations, another really cool idea I first observed by an exceptional facilitator. Joey would create expectations for the class AND for himself as the facilitator. He would engage the group in a discussion to identify expectations/ground rules for the class, but then he would open it up to the class and ask, "What would you expect from me during our time together?"

This was such a cool idea to gain buy-in from the class to keep them focused and affords him the opportunity, if needed, to refer back to the list throughout the session if things were getting off track. It immediately created a partnership bond between him and his class.

There are a lot of nuances when it comes to starting your session effectively and by integrating the DAGR method, you will not only set your session up for success, but your audience will be primed for success as well.

Activity Cycle

I'd like to take a stroll down memory lane with you. When you reflect back on your professional career, what is the first legitimate new hire class you remember attending as a learner? I am not referencing the situations where you are sat down next to a tenured person and that is your "new hire" training. An actual training class with a trainer.

Can you recall some of the other people in the class? What did the room look like? Were there computers? Was it well lit? Do you remember who you sat beside?

Who was your trainer?

Now that we have those memories fresh in our brains, I want you to think about the overall experience. Was it enjoyable? Do you recall doing any type of activities?

These activities may have been completing worksheets, scavenger hunts, group work, role plays, etc.

In thinking through those activities, do you remember leaning over to your "neighbor" sitting next to you and asking, "Do you know what we're supposed to be doing?"

If you have never been in a situation that you've never had to ask your neighbor that question, you are in rare company.

It happens a lot when an audience is asked to complete a task and the person leading the session has such a deep understanding of what needs to be completed, they lose sight of the fact that this is the first time this audience has seen this. Directions are fired off, timers are started, and audience members are left confused.

I am guilty of this.

When I first started training, I had to invest additional time into activities because I was not being as clear with the directions I was providing and the class continued to ask questions or started to complete the activity how they felt it needed to be completed, even if it wasn't exactly the way it was supposed to be completed.

This is why having a process on how to facilitate activities is a separator between good and great presenters/facilitators.

If you have never utilized an actual process facilitating activities before, you are likely having a similar reaction as I did when I was first introduced to using one. I did not understand why a process is needed. I thought, you give them directions, they do the activity, and then you're done.

When I had that thought, I learned quickly I was very wrong.

The Activity Cycle is designed to add structure to your activities, so your audience gets the most out of their experience, they are able to apply what they learn, and it creates efficiency for you so you don't have to repeat instructions over and over.

iDARED - the Activity Cycle.

- Instruct
- Demo
- Attendee Summary
- Recap & Go
- Explore
- Debrief

These steps will help ensure each of your activities has a higher rate of success and it ensures your attendees know what they are being asked to complete.

Instruct

This step is where you as the facilitator will outline the instructions for the activity, including what success looks like. The majority of the time, if you are facilitating a class with a Facilitator Guide that was created by an Instructional Designer, instructions will already be included.

A key on this step is to balance the complexity of the instructions. If there are more than three simple steps for the activity, the instructions will need to be available for reference for the audience. This could mean they are posted on a slide that remains visible throughout the activity. You may end up preparing an easel sheet ahead of time to post within the room. Another option is the instructions may be included in the participant materials. As long as the audience can follow along while you provide the instructions and refer back to them during the activity, it will aid in their accurate completion of the activity.

Something else to consider in the Instruct portion of the Activity Cycle is if the instructions for the activity are more than 10 bullets long, you may need to break the activity into two different activities. If the activity is too complex, then your likelihood of folks getting lost and struggling to complete the activity goes up significantly.

Demo

This step is designed to enhance confidence for the learners to better understand what they are to complete by the end of the activity. It may not be a step that is needed every time, but the reinforcement can help mitigate questions during the activity.

If you are having the group complete a knowledge quiz and your instructions outline there is 15 minutes to complete the quiz, the quiz is located in system, and there are 12 questions in total. In a situation like this, it does not make any sense to do a Demo.

The purpose of the Demo is it allows the audience to see how the activity should be completed, and/or successful completion.

One of the most common activities where a Demo adds immense value is with Role Plays. These are the activities, which are very common for any role that requires client interactions, when there are three audience members working together. One person would be the client, one would be the company representative, and the third person would be the observer. They put on their "imagination hats" and the individuals playing the client and company representative interact based on the scenario provided. The third person observes the interaction and takes notes based on the established criteria (e.g. quality metrics) then provides feedback on the interaction.

Needless to say, there are a lot of moving pieces within the activity and since you are asking adults to put on their "imagination hats" there is an inherit fear of looking silly. A Demo can ease some of the anxiety.

The Demo can operate in two different ways:

1. Facilitator demonstrates what success looks like, or
2. Obtain volunteers from the audience to help demonstrate.

Both instances can be successful.

Attendee Summary

The Attendee Summary is to ensure the class has a strong understanding of the instructions. This can be accomplished by asking 1-3 questions around the specific directions provided in the Instruct step.

For instance,

- "How much time do we have?"
- "What is the list you are creating?"
- "What are the roles each person will be playing?"

Although this may seem redundant, however the purpose with this step is to ensure the audience can recall key instructions for the activity, especially those instructions that are crucial (e.g. time to complete the activity).

You will want to keep your Attendee Summary to no more than 1-3 follow-up questions.

Recap & Go

This step is the shortest of them all. This is a quick reminder of 1-2 key instructions, then sending them to the activity.

For instance:

- "I look forward to hearing about what you learned from your customer role play. See you in 10 minutes."

The above example achieves two recaps for a role play activity. You may also notice it is incorporated into common language. It is not intended to be a list, just casual, quick reminders that you want imprinted in the front of the brains of your audience as they launch into the activity.

Explore

This step is designed to ensure learning is taking place. It also affords you the opportunity to provide correction if a person/group is off track for achieving the result of the activity.

During Explore, you have the opportunity to reaffirm and verbally acknowledge great work being completed during the activity.

IMPORTANT: Activity time is not Trainer break time. Too many times, I have seen facilitators feel they can take a break while activities are taking place. As the leader of the session, it is your obligation to remain engaged in the learning.

When the activity starts, taking a casual stroll throughout the room with your ears open, you can observe the interactions amongst audience members, you get to hear how individuals and groups are thinking, you get to easily answer questions, and you can reinforce concepts.

Being around the audience during the Explore phase, not only allows you to observe, but most importantly, it allows you to better connect with your audience. Even showing interest in their work and providing a smile or reaffirming head nod when they're on the right track is very impactful for audiences.

One thing I want to callout, that I've heard before, especially during presentations. If you are presenting from an actual stage and you turn your audience loose to do an exercise, don't be the presenter that thinks, "But I'm on the stage and I need to stay on the stage."

GET YOUR ASS OFF THE STAGE!!! Find a way.

If you want to be remembered for creating an exceptional experience, you will find a way to Explore the room and engage with the audience. You add even more impact when you tell them you're coming during the Recap & Go.

> "Once I start the timer for 15 minutes, I am going to be moving around because I want to hear the great things you're coming up with."

That adds a ton of credibility to you as the presenter or facilitator.

Debrief

This is the magic step. This is when you get to ensure learning took place. In most cases, the session material (e.g. facilitator guide) has built in training debrief questions to ask the learners. These questions are targeted to ensure the key deliverables are achieved.

It is also the responsibility of the facilitator/presenter to adjust depending on the class. These kinds of adjustments may come from what was observed during the Explore step.

If a particular group did really well, acknowledge you heard them doing well and have them share with the class their learnings.

If a group/person struggled with the activity, get a sense if they had a "light bulb" moment when you were able to guide them back on track. Tread lightly here because you don't want to put someone in the spotlight if they struggled and didn't have a lightbulb moment with the activity. While you are engaging with them during Explore, you will know whether they made it past the struggle spot. If they did, highlight where they got stuck and either highlight how they overcame it, or even better, have them highlight how they overcame that struggle spot.

The length of your Debrief will depend on the length of the activity. Timing wise, it doesn't make a lot of sense to complete a 20-minute Debrief for a 5-minute activity. However, there is a caveat here. When you start diving into the Debrief and the audience is engaging in the discussion and you can see true learning is occurring, it is your job to let that conversation breathe. If the audience is connecting the activity to how they can apply it on the job, and brainstorming how it will make them better, let them continue that journey.

I'd recommend that while this is occurring, remain engaged and you will need to be assessing where additional time can be made up later so you can stay on track with your agenda time.

Example of an Activity Cycle

To help provide insight into how this could work from start to finish, I will give you an example of how this would look.

Activity Scenario: Facilitating a leadership class with 20 front line managers and they are going to be placed into groups to brainstorm ideas of how they could address the scenarios listed in the materials using "ABC Conversation Model." (Note: The conversation model is fictious and below is how I would set up the activity)

Ok, so we spent some time talking through our ABC Conversation Model, now let's spend some time figuring out how we can apply this model in different scenarios.

Here's what we are going to do:

(**Instruct**) First, on page 28 of your guide, you will see a list of three common situations that can occur for us as leaders. You will work with your partner, preferably someone you have not had a chance to work with yet.

You and your partner will read the scenarios and brainstorm together how you would apply the ABC Conversation Model for each scenario. You will have 15 minutes to document in your guide how you would approach each scenario. After the 15 minutes, we will review the scenarios and get 1-2 examples from different groups for each scenario.

(**Demo**) Before I start the timer, let's look at a quick example. On the slide, you see an example where two of your Associates recently had a very heated conversation over implementing the XYZ process.

Based on this example, what are some of your thoughts as to how we can apply the ABC Model? (participants share ideas)

What we just did by talking through how we'd apply the model in this scenario is the same conversation you will have with your partner.

(**Attendee Summary**) How long do you have to complete the scenario with your partner?
   What model are we using to address the scenarios?

Wonderful! What questions to you have before we start?

(**Recap & Go**) I look forward to hearing what you come up with. Take your 15 minutes.

(**Explore** by moving throughout the room)

(**Debrief**) Our time is up. I heard some great conversations and ideas for applying the ABC Model. Let's take a look at each scenario and hear ideas of how some of you would incorporate the ABC Conversation Model.

When you see the process mapped out, even in text, it should give you an idea as to how the Activity Cycle can be applied. It is not intended to be complicated, however where I have seen folks get stuck in applying this process is because it is a process. The stress kicks in by worrying about hitting each step. It takes repetition.

The easiest step to apply is the Instruct step, and that is because you're likely already doing this step in your sessions.

The Demo step is one that has been easy for folks to do, especially when you're familiar with the content. The hard part is remembering to do it, if it's needed.

Attendees Summary and Recap & Go steps are the ones most struggle with because they are unfamiliar to most. When you look at the example provided, you'll notice they are not complicated, but because it is likely a new concept is why it is hard. It will feel awkward at first, yet doing these steps ensures you know your audience is aware of key instructions and it is at the front of their mind before the activity starts.

I've always enjoyed the Explore step because it gives me the opportunity to see learning being applied and I get to engage more with the audience.

With the importance of the Debrief, make sure the time is not shortened too much and your questions are targeted to ensure the learning took place.

Executing the Activity Cycle takes practice. You may find yourself writing out the different steps in your notes or guide to ensure the experience for your audience is enhanced. Once you've utilized the process several times, eventually it will become a habit.

Question Types

Questions are to a facilitator/presenter as a hammer is to a carpenter. It is a tool that every toolbox should possess.

Facilitators will use a lot more questions than a presenter because they are driving two-way communication and engagement. Yet, some of the best presenters will incorporate questions very strategically within their presentation, especially if they want to make the experience for their audience real.

In his TED Talk, "The Art of Misdirection," Apollo Robbins closes his presentation with the question, "If you could control someone's attention, what would you do with it?"

He did not solicit responses from the audience, like a facilitator might, but he wanted to leave a lasting impression with a thought-provoking question. He wanted to make it real for his audience.

There are four types of questions that I have used that has helped me engage my audiences and I refer to them as LOAD questions.

1. Leading
2. Overhead
3. Assumptive
4. Direct

Leading

These questions are great to narrow the responses, almost like a multiple-choice question. For instance, "Based on what we just covered, would you choose A or B?" This can also be beneficial in guiding learners to choose the correct response by making the other option glaringly incorrect.

An example that has a glaring difference would be, "Would you rather run a mile carrying, a bag full of feathers or a bag full of bowling balls?"

Leading questions are a great way to get more quiet attendees to participate. Engaging them with an option that is obvious, it is great way to get the quiet folks "out of their shell." Not only does it help to get quiet audience member to open up, but it is a great way to build up confidence. When they get the question right, giving that person praise can enhance their experience and confidence.

Overhead

One of the most common question types utilized by facilitators is Overhead questions. These questions are the ones that are asked to the entire audience. Overhead questions are a great way to engage an audience toward the beginning of a session. This opens the opportunity for anyone to answer the question.

Ninja trick: if you are asking overhead questions and the same 1-2 participants are "question hoggers," you can ask an overhead question to another portion of the room which opens for others to participate but limits the "question hoggers."

"Question Hoggers" are the attendees are the ones that immediately start speaking after a question is asked and doesn't allow time for others to answer the question.

Assumptive

This is the question type that gets people nodding and engaged in a way that the answer is completely obvious. For instance, "Wouldn't you like to be the best public speaker you can be?"

The negative response assumptive question can even be powerful. Sales professionals utilize a similar tactic to get clients saying "no" to obvious statements so the solution you're pitching sounds more elegant, thusly lowering the potential client's defenses.

The same applies to presenters/facilitators. "Quick show of hands, who would love to be in front of an audience and due to fear, pee their pants?" Absolutely absurd, right?

Yet, when a question like that is posed, no one will raise their hands. And an absurd question like that is an easy way to inject some humor.

Direct

These are the questions are that are asked directly to an audience member. I have seen Facilitators try to gravitate away from using these out of fear of intimidating someone. I've even been told, "I won't use direct questions because it's not fair to them."

There is a risk of that, BUT (please notice the big but) when in front of an audience it is our job as facilitators and presenters to read the audience. We must be attuned to know when and how to engage attendees with a direct question.

Direct questions have been one of the most impactful question types I have used with audience members. By getting to know audience members, you start to identify some of their backgrounds and possible areas of expertise. This is when I heavily lean into Direct questions.

Here's an example, if someone in the session has experience with the system being covered in the session, during a certain portion of the session, either based on the content or a discussion, I may pose the question, "Joe, I know you've utilized this system before, how have you handled this previously?"

The other great benefit of Direct questions is if someone is very quiet or possibly struggling with confidence, asking a Direct question, especially one you know they can answer, you now have the opportunity to boost their confidence. After they respond to the question, you can say, "Well done! I knew you'd have what we were looking for." This can lead to them contributing more.

Ninja trick: the safest direct question to ask is an opinion-based question.

This means you allow the participant to safely answer a question where there is no wrong answer. For instance, "Jack, in your opinion, what is the procedure we need to follow here?" Even if they don't provide the exact answer you're looking for, they are still not wrong because it was their opinion.

If an incorrect answer is provided, you can still protect their ego. "I can see where you're going with that, and in this particular circumstance, we would need to follow XYZ steps."

Pro Tip: To help ensure a participant is not taken off guard and making the defensive, add a slight pause after saying their name.

For instance, "Jack, (pause) in your opinion, what is the procedure we need to follow here?" This allows the learner to hear their name and avert their focus to you.

Utilizing LOAD question types will allow you the ability to keep your audience engaged while ensuring you have the opportunity to check for understanding.

Tackling Questions Process

When I first learned about having a process about how to effectively receive questions, I was dumbfounded. Why would there be a process? Someone asks a question, you answer it…simple. I'd imagine you had a very similar thought when you read that header.

HOWEVER, what I learned is the successful addressing of a question leans heavily into the Audience Experience.

Have you ever encountered a situation where someone asked you a question after answering the question, the other person claims, "that is not what I was asking."

Perhaps you have been stumped by a question.

Having a process can successfully position you to create an engaging experience for your audience and ensure the question is addressed to the "askers" satisfaction.

It is important to note, I didn't just say Answer the question, more on that later.

Here is the process:

1. Listen
2. Recap
3. Resolve
4. Verify

Listen

This first step is where the two listening "devices" on the side of your noggin (ears) get put to work. You will want to give the person asking the question your undivided attention.

Be careful not to start thinking about what you are going to say while they are asking, you may miss something. This can be tough especially if you've trained the same session several times and you likely can anticipate certain questions. Then if you add to the fact there are times when we have an audience member that attempts to provide their entire life story with a question that is buried in there somewhere. (Yes, that may sound rough, but if you've spent a fair amount of time in front of an audience, you are smiling right now because you know what I'm talking about.) The point is regardless of the quality of the question, or the length, you need to remain focused on the question. The reason is it sets you up to successfully address the question being asked.

During the Listen step, it is a great time to incorporate some non-verbal listening queues:

- Nodding
- Smiling/smirking
- Raising of eyebrows to show interest
- Even moving a little closer to the person asking, even if only a couple steps in his/her general location

These subtle cues demonstrate to the individual asking the question that you are engaged in the question they are asking.

Recap

After Listening, you will want to demonstrate that you heard the question. The Recap is the step of repeating, or paraphrasing, the question so the person that asked the question knows you understood the question.

Examples of effective ways to Recap are:

- "If I understood you correctly, you're asking…"
- "Just to confirm, you asked… right?"
- "For those that may not have heard, the question was…"

There are many ways to Recap a question and as you become more comfortable with this process, you will find the applicable way that works best for you, especially that aligns with your authenticity.

Over the years of using this process, this is the step that is the most foreign and will feel the most awkward in the beginning phases of implementing. This is also the step when you begin utilizing it, that will make it sound like you are following a process. Through repetition, it will eventually be part of how you communicate overall. Which this process works really well in meetings.

Pro-Tip:
   As you continue to refine this process, you can eventually Recap the question as you answer it. For instance, if someone were to ask you "Why is the sky blue," you could paraphrase (Recap) the question into your response. "The sky is blue because…"

This confirms with the person that asked the question that you heard and understood their question, it sounds more natural, and it maintains a conversational tone with your session.

Bonus:

If you really want to amplify the experience of your audience with how you address questions, add an acknowledgment during your Recap. This acknowledgment could be as simple as:

- "Thank you for asking."
- "I was really hoping that question would come up."
- "Wonderful"
- "Great"

It's important to note with the last two examples, I didn't mention, "Wonderful question," or "Great question." This is a common trap presenters and facilitators fall into. They begin quantifying questions. "Great question" is the most common response you will hear, yet if you use that all the time then shift to "Wonderful question," it is possible the previous folks may wonder why their question wasn't wonderful. If you have the habit already of saying, "Great question," the easiest adjustment is to cut "question" off of the end.

Resolve

When I think of the various steps in the process for tackling questions, Resolve is the most exciting. The excitement around the Resolve step is because there are a variety of different ways to tackle or address a question. It can be very simple, yet you can weave a web of engagement centered around each question.

Let's take a look at the various ways to **Resolve** questions. We will start with the easiest.

Answer it - if you are able to answer the question correctly, do it.

Parking Lot it - If it is a question you don't have an answer to, you can place it in a Parking Lot. A Parking Lot is a place in the room where questions are captured that require follow-up. The common practice is to dedicate a portion of a dry erase board or an easel sheet that is labeled with "Parking Lot" and is used to capture questions that can't be answered in the moment. The reason this is helpful, especially in training sessions, is it keeps the questions captured visibly for the audience. The key with Parking Lots is ensure you follow-up, no matter what, even if it is an email to the entire group after the session is over. You've worked so hard to establish credibility and not following up will diminish that.

Reverse it - This tactic is where you can send the question back to the person that asked the question. Reversing the question has to be assessed and positioned correctly. The reason it has to be positioned correctly is because there is a risk that if you reverse it, the person asking may respond, "That's why I asked you." UGH! That is why assessing where the person is in their knowledge and willingness to play along. The safest avenue is to ask an opinion-based question. "With your question about _____, in your opinion, how do you think you'd handle it?" Keep in mind, no matter how delicately you position the question, you may still get the "that's why I asked" response. If that occurs, accept it (e.g. "no worries") and continue to Resolve the question another way.

Relay it - This is the option to send the question to someone else in the audience. You can open up to the rest of the audience or direct it to another individual, especially if you know there is expertise in the session that can answer the question. This can be a fun way to add levity to the session. When I relay questions, I will ask the person from where the question originated, "Thanks for that question. What do you think if we "phone-a-friend" on this one?"

Empower it - This option is one where you direct the audience to find the answer. This option could add time dedicated to resolving a question, either during the session or after. Ultimately, if you get a question that would be very valuable for everyone to learn, you can empower the audience to find the answer themselves. An example might be if you get a process specific question. If you know the audience has access to systems where they can find the answer themselves, you can ask the entire audience to locate the answer in the system. By leveraging this tactic, you would be building confidence for the audience to be self-sufficient once they leave your session. You can even give homework for the audience to research before the next session and report back to everyone what they found out. Peer-to-peer learning is a powerful tool.

Now that we have an idea of the various ways to Resolve a question, this is where things get fun. Depending on the question, you can start to utilize combinations of the different tactics.

With Reverse and Relay, these are both designed to increase engagement opportunities of the entire audience. You may be in a situation to leverage both with one question. For instance, if you Reverse it back to the person asking and they provide an answer, or even if they say, "I don't know," you can then Relay to the rest of the group.

Another possible combination could be to relay the question to the group and if they are unable to answer the question, you can either answer it yourself, or you can empower them to find the answer.

Pro Tip: When utilizing Relay or Reverse to resolve a question, you want to ensure you maintain a level of credibility. You do this by "adding your two cents." This means that after you get a response from either of these concepts, you want to engage the question. You could add something like "I agree" or "Love what you mentioned, and I would add one extra item." Both are examples to keep you in the driver seat of credibility and avoid doubt from creeping into the minds of your audience that you don't know or are avoiding questions.

Verify: The final step in the sequence is to validate or confirm if the answer(s) met the expectations of the person that asked the original question. It is putting the pretty little bow on the question package.

Examples could include:

- "Does that help?"
- "Does that answer your question?"
- "Cool?"
- "How'd we do?"

The last two examples are questions that may seem a little odd and perhaps felt awkward to read. I added them as those are a couple of the examples I use when I am working with an audience. They fit with my delivery style and my authenticity.

With this last step of the Tackling Questions process, no matter how you position your follow-up with the person asking the question, the goal is to ensure you connect with that person to ensure they feel satisfied with the outcome, which should be achieved in the Resolve step.

Putting It All Together

Now that you've seen the framework, below is a start to finish example of the full process in action. I will use an actual question that I've received during a leadership class I was facilitating.

> -Audience Member: *"What are some examples or strategies you've used to improve engagement within a team, more specifically improving engagement scores?" (Listen)*

−Me: "Just to confirm, you're looking a few ideas to enhance engagement, possibly to help you and your team?" (Recap)

−Audience Member: "Exactly"

−Me: "Wonderful! (Recap-Acknowledge) I am so glad this came because engagement strategies can be tough to implement. I have a couple ideas, but are you ok if we check with the rest of the group to hear what's worked for them?"

−Audience Member: "Sure"

−Me: "Let's hear from some of you, what have been some strategies you have used to have an engaged team?" (Relay)

(received responses from a few other members of the audience)

−Me: "I love these ideas. The recognition idea we heard is one that can really be valuable for teams. For me, when I've led teams, the best engagement strategy comes down to three things: Communication, Development, and Care. Teams need consistent communication, they need the opportunity to develop or grow in their role, and they need to know you care about them as a person, not just a worker. How I've achieved each of those has varied by team, but those are always the foundation in which I ensure the teams I've led get the most from me. [Resolve] Does that help give you some ideas? (Verify)

Although it may seem weird as if you're reading a transcript, but you can see it is possible to seamlessly incorporate the Tackling Questions process without it sounding like you're following a process.

If you really want to become great at utilizing this process, practice everywhere. You will learn quickly how to incorporate the steps without if sounding like you are following a process. Practice it in meetings, one-on-ones, water cooler conversations. I've even challenged people to use when going through a drive-thru. The true test of your mastery of this process will come if you can utilize this process while having a conversation with your significant other. There is no better place for true unadulterated feedback than the person in which you share your life. Speaking from experience, you will refine this skill quickly.

Power Closings

An audience will usually remember the last impression in which you left them. If you rush to beat the clock to end on time, your audience will leave with a sense of feeling rushed and perhaps feel incomplete. If you abruptly end your session, your audience will leave with a sense of confusion. If you focus on a quality closing for your session, your audience will walk away accomplished, possibly inspired, and will fondly remember their time with you as well spent.

There are three truths I have learned throughout my career in front of audience:

1. Audiences remember the first impression
2. Audiences remember how you made them feel throughout (supported)
3. Audiences remember the final impression

This is why a Power Closing can be such a treasured asset.

Before diving into how to structure a Power Closing, there are two seeds I want to plant in the back of your mind as you're learning about this concept.

- Keep your closing succinct and focused.

- Make the closing impactful.

When considering the length of a closing, it will ultimately be determined by the length of your session. The sweet spot when planning your closing is 5-10% of the total run time of your session. For instance, a six-hour class is 360 minutes, which means your Power Closing should not exceed 36 minutes. That doesn't mean you HAVE to dedicate 36 minutes for your closing, it is important you don't exceed that time. For a six-hour session, I would normally gravitate more toward the 18-minute mark (5%). It is more succinct and if planned correctly, you can cover quality elements of a Power Closing within that window.

It is important to make sure the closing is impactful. If a class invested six hours of their time, help them understand what they learned/achieved and how their newfound knowledge will benefit them, whether in their personal growth or professional career.

These two things will add "stickiness" to your last impression with your audience.

Elements of Power Closings

As we dive into the elements of Power Closings, the intent is not to dictate a specific process to follow, it is designed to equip you with tools from which to choose so you can customize a closing for any session you lead.

With the list of elements below, to achieve a true Power Closing, you should include 2-4 elements in every closing. If your closing is shorter, then two should suffice, and yet if structured appropriately an 8-minute close could include four elements.

Here are the elements of Power Closings:

1. Restate Value (WIIFM)
2. Restate Objectives
3. Revisit Roadmap/Agenda
4. Power Quote
5. Refresh Parking Lot Questions
6. Audience Commitments
7. Emphasize Key Learnings
8. On The Job Application
9. Challenge Them

Restate Value (WIIFM)

The Value reviewed during your Strong Opening, can be reiterated. The WIIFM is why they should care about what you are covered during your session. This can serve a reminder of the value the in which the session was designed.

How this can look:

With the notes or guide you use for your session, you likely have the value statement or WIIFM highlighted, bolded, circled, or underlined. You can reiterate that value in a simple statement as you wrap up. "If you think back to when we started our time together, we mentioned this session was designed to do _____, now that we are wrapping up, are you able to see how this can improve your _____?"

Restate Objectives

The objectives of a course are the "goals," what you set out to achieve in the session. The good news is if you are facilitating content that was built by an Instructional Designer there will be objectives built into the course. Be mindful, that Objectives that are built by Instructional Designers are reviewed in the beginning and it can be valuable for your audience for them revisit what they achieved within the session.

How this can look:

Copying the Objective slide from the opening and placing it at the end of the presentation then stating, "We set out to achieve..." (going one by one)... "How'd we do?"

Asking the final question allows the audience to acknowledge the session achieved its goal for them. It is also a way to confirm with the audience if they felt the accomplished something.

Revisit the Roadmap (Agenda)

Learners can appreciate seeing how far they've come throughout a training. Simply going back to the start of the journey and recalling the path taken can help the learners obtain a level of success by seeing how far they journeyed.

How this can look:

You can copy and paste the agenda slide at the end of your presentation, or if you have it written out on an easel sheet, you can refer to the agenda, "Today we covered...".

Power Quote

The easy part is it can be a really good way to end on an inspiring note and is quick to cover. The hard part is finding a quote that connects to the learning and the audience. Having a random quote that doesn't connect can leave your audience confused as to why it's referenced. There have been times I needed to add a little bit of context to the quote, especially if it was one I really like, but just be careful having to dedicate a lot of time explaining the quote as it will eat up unnecessary time in your succinct closing.

How this can look:

The quote can be posted in a couple different places. It could be on your final slide, it could be something you write out on an easel sheet or dry erase board, or there are times when the quote may be added in the participant material. You can simply set up the quote as you transition to it, "As I think about this course and everything we've covered, I like the quote by ..."

Refresh Parking Lot Questions

As mentioned previously, it is ok not to have all the answers during a session, this is where a Parking Lot can be valuable. The Parking Lot is the repository or list of questions that surfaced during the session that either could not be answered or were not applicable to the subject matter. If you have Parking Lot questions that were captured during the session, it is helpful to revisit the questions captured. Then commit to follow-up based on what you were able to find out.

Ninja trick: following up on Parking Lot questions can be a great way to stay top of mind, remain credible, and quite possibly increase session feedback responses.

How this can look:

You can physically move over to the space where the Parking Lot questions were captured, then simply review the questions. "When we look at the questions captured in our Parking Lot we have _____, I will send an update within the next two days so all of you have the answers we were unable to address during the session."

It's good to note I mentioned "update" instead of "provide answers." This is intentional as there may be situations where you may not get all the answers to the questions within the timeframe in which you're committing. However, by sending an update, you can provide some answers, if you have them, and letting the group know the progress being made to finding the answers.

Audience Commitments

Gaining commitments from the attendees can be powerful. Dedicating time at the end of the session allows the audience time to reflect. They will be able to contemplate those key points that were covered during your session that will help them be better than they were before they walked into your session.

Be sure to dedicate time for the learners to actually put pen to paper. If it is a virtual session, they will likely type them, however the physical act of writing out the commitments with a pen on a piece of paper aids in accountability and makes it more personal for them. With any goal from a session, we want the gained knowledge and/or skill to become permanent with our audiences, otherwise why should they come. Adding that extra level of personal accountability is a huge step to making things permanent for your audiences.

You may have covered a litany of valuable topics throughout your session, and it would be unfair, not to mention unpractical, to ask the audience members to write down all of their takeaways. The intent with Audience Commitments is to have them write down 1-2 items they feel they can commit to upon the conclusion of the session.

How this can look:

"Grab a pen and a piece of paper and take the next three minutes to right down what you feel you can immediately apply as soon as you leave this session today."

When you are setting up the time for them to write down their commitments, you can let them know, "once everyone has their 1-2 items, I would like to hear from a couple of you on what you wrote down." This adds just an extra opportunity to make the commitments permanent by verbalizing them. If you have audience members share what they wrote down, it is a good practice to add simple acknowledgements, "Thank you for sharing those, it sounds like you've identified some great ideas to apply in your role."

Emphasize Key Learnings

Somewhat akin to Learner Commitments, this is covering key learnings, the difference is covering key learning for which the material was designed to achieve. This can be somewhat aligned with the Objectives, but it is focusing on various learnings that aided in achieving the objectives.

Being familiar with the content and as you've led the session, you will know the main points to review. The main points could be refreshing the audience one last time on a new process flow, especially if it's an acronym. It could also be revisiting a great discussion about a particular topic that took place with this particular audience.

How this can look:

When you incorporate this component in your closing, it doesn't have to be an elaborate plan or set-up. It is simply revisiting certain topics that you want them to be reminded of one last time. "If we think back to everything we talked about today, there were three main things we covered today: 1).... 2)... 3)..., does that sound familiar?"

On the Job Application

With any type of session you deliver, the ability for adult learners to apply what they've learned is the ultimate goal. It is the difference between knowing theory and practical application. This element is the close sister to Learner Commitments and Restate Value. All three are focused on what audience members will get from the session, which is usually connected to their ability to perform better in their roles.

For this particular element, instead of highlighting only the value of the session or driving the commitment from the audience, you will reiterate how the audience can apply their newfound knowledge to their job. This could be remaining compliant with a new process, enhanced customer interactions, or creating better audience experiences. This can go on as the application will be dependent on the session you're delivering.

How this can look:

Since the On-the-Job Application is closely tied to two of the other elements, it allows for an easy parlay within your closing. For instance, after you review the Learner Commitments and you hear some examples from your audience you can mention, "it is wonderful to hear many of your ideas as to how you can start applying what you've learned. We heard from Joe when he mentioned and we heard from Mary and her focus on which are fantastic examples. I want to make sure that regardless of what you begin applying first, taking and integrating it daily, you will become more efficient, and your customer interaction will improve as well."

Challenge Them

Offering a challenge can provide the nudge most learners may need. This can be impactful if attendees have competitive behaviors. Challenging the audience members can be a creative challenge for presenters and facilitators. The reason this can be a challenge for us is we want to ensure it is something that will excite the audience to act.

For instance, if I were to issue a challenge at the end of a class covering the content in this book, I would state, "I want to challenge to find just ONE thing we have covered today and apply it in your next interaction with another human. Whether it is in your next meeting, your next presentation, or even your next visit to a drive thru."

The reason a challenge can be valuable is it can not only get an audience excited, but you can tap into the competitive nature of your audience. Yes, there are people that may say, "I'm not a competitive person." That may be true, yet there are very few humans that don't like to be the first to do something.

How this can look:

Issuing a challenge and providing an opportunity to shine is something most adults will strive for. "The last thing I will leave you with today is a challenge. I want to challenge this group to take our new customer interaction model and apply it on your next call with a customer. Then in your next team huddle, I want you to be the first person to share how the interaction went and what you learned from applying it. I've already chatted with your managers, and they are very eager to see who the first person will be to apply it and share what they learned in the next team huddle."

Those are all the elements that you have at your disposal when you are crafting your Power Closing. Although when you look at a list of nine things, remember you only need to utilize 2-4 in each of your closings. This provides you options. I also want to challenge you to review the list again and pick out the two that resonate with you the most and in the next session you deliver, incorporate those two elements. Your audience may not realize it, but they will most certainly appreciate the lasting positive impression you made with them.

Reading the Room

In 2018, I was asked to come to Chicago to deliver a Change Management course for a group mid to upper-level leaders (Managers, Sr Managers, & Directors) for an organization that I had done a fair amount of work with previously. I had met and worked with most of them previously and since I had worked with them before I knew they were a good group, and we would have some fun through the day long training.

Everything I anticipated was coming true. They were participating. They were asking questions. They were engaged. Then came the point in the afternoon when the energy completely plummeted. It was the perfect circumstance for disaster. It was after lunch and everyone's bellies were full. Then when coupled with the fact that the way the course was designed, the afternoon was very PowerPoint heavy. Essentially a lot of slides and a lot of me talking.

I felt the energy dropping. Audience members were leaning further back in their chairs, some were even somewhat slouching. Heads were resting on palms. I believe one person was one flap of a duck's wing away from falling asleep. I knew I had to move quickly otherwise this highly engaged group was not going to have the experience I'd set out to achieve.

About halfway through a slide, I told the group, "You know what, we've seen quite a few slides already, let's do something a little different."

In the moment, I pivoted the content delivery from PowerPoint slides to a Gallery Walk. A Gallery Walk is a tactic Facilitators will utilize by posting topics, usually with easel sheets, at various points around the room. Then the audience is then divided up and assigned to different topics. They are then asked to brainstorm ideas based on the content/topics on each sign.

They capture a variety of ideas then after a prescribed amount of time, the groups rotate to the next topic on a different sheet. This cycle repeats until each group have a chance to add to each topic throughout the room. Once that occurs the facilitator will review each of the sheets with the class and engage in a discussion to share the various perspectives captured.

Pivoting in the moment and most importantly getting the group moving when the energy level dropped through the floor was valuable. The group returned to the levels of engagement and participation they had when the day started.

When working to create a great audience experience, the ability to successfully read the room is crucial.

Reading the room is the ability to:

- Feel the energy level of the audience.
- Watch for disengaged behaviors.
- Willingness to learn more.

Feel the Energy Level of the Audience

Once you've been in front of an audience several times, you become attuned to the energy of the class. Sometimes you can actually see eyes start to get heavy (e.g. falling asleep), but you actually can feel it.

There are times when are you are doing the lion's share of sparking energy into the room. Depending on the audience, that may be required. This is evident when you ask a question and there is nothing but blank stares being returned.

Ideas to Overcome Low energy:

- Call an audible on the agenda and send the class for an unscheduled break.
- Pause your content to have everyone stand up. You can take the class through some very basic stretches to get the blood flowing again.
- Pivot to a quick energizer activity, preferably one that is closely related to session objectives.

If low energy is not addressed, your session could end with an unfortunate "thud" as it falls to the floor.

Watch for Disengaged Behaviors

A dangerous trap for facilitators and presenters is to try and power through the content regardless as to whether the audience is following. This then becomes a "check the box" activity and not an experience.

Disengaged behaviors may be when audience members are checking phones/laptops, sitting back in chair with arms crossed, or possibly looking out the window/Daydreaming.

Ideas to overcome disengaged behaviors:

- Pause and Check-in

At this point you can pause the content you're delivering and ask to see what questions the audience is thinking of now. This can be a simply stating, "Hey folks, we've covered a lot so far, I want to pause for a moment to see what types of questions are coming to mind." (Notice the assumptive open-ended question.)

Then depending on the responses or questions you can continue to move forward with the content, yet if you are still seeing tired faces or not receiving questions, then it might be time for a content break.

- Content Break

A content break can be a simple redirection and engage the group for a simple activity. This may be as simple as saying, "I want to pause briefly since we are past the halfway point, I would like each of you to write down one thing that has resonated with you thus far. I'll give you three minutes. At the end of the three minutes, I would like to hear from at least five of you on what you wrote down."

This can be valuable to help you gauge the level of understanding and if you are still moving toward achieving the objectives of your session. You may find that a content break may be to give the group an ad-hoc break. These don't have to be long, even 3-5 minutes, but that little bit of time gives your audience the mental break they may need.

- Give Them Something to Do

This can not only get them doing something, instead of listening to you, but it also allows you to see if they are tracking with key concepts from your session. Similar to the content break its reengaging different parts of their brain and body in the participation of your session. In addition to writing down of what has resonated with them up to that point, you can give them something extra to do by asking them to get up from their chair and find someone at another table and share what they wrote down.

This gets their bodies moving and the extra blood flow can reinvigorate them. This is also helpful when addressing the resistant person that is leaning back in their chair with their arms crossed. More than likely they are not enjoying the experience and possibly waiting to be impressed.

Willingness to Learn More

When you see this in an audience, it is a great feeling. This is when learners are sitting forward in their seats, making consistent eye contact, and give you positive non-verbal signs (e.g. raised eyebrows, nodding along with your points, and smiling).

As a facilitator/presenter, it is awesome to ride the wave of eager learners. It can be a great confidence boost for you. When you are seeing this occur, you know you are hitting your sweet spot.

There are two things in which to be mindful when you have the eager learners. It is rare when an entire audience attending your session is a room full of engaged learners. This can be due to multitasking, told they had to attend, or any variety of human dynamics that influence audience members state of mind. When you see the attendees that are engaged, try to avoid tailoring your session to those that are showing up the most.

Due to the confidence boost we get from these attendees; it is natural to want to maintain that good feeling. Then we want to keep feeding that momentum, yet what that can do is can drive strong disengagement with other attendees that are not as eager. Nothing is worse than getting feedback on a survey that states, "I don't think he knew I was there." UGH! Talk about your epic gut punch. By that time, it is too late to do anything about it.

The other thing in which to be mindful is you don't ride the eager learner wave for too long. If you've been to a beach you've seen all waves eventually crash into the shore. If you keep pushing too hard because there is great engagement, even from just a few, it is easy to want to keep things going because you feel the class is getting it. Before you know, you've blown past break times. Be sure to still allow for brain breaks or breaks in general. Even the most eager of learners can, and will, get tired and need to recharge.

The Audience Experience can be complicated to achieve because as you've seen there are a number of "tools" to utilize. If these are brand new to you, it will certainly take time to get acclimated.

Here are a couple tips to help get you started:

1. **One bite at a time** - with any new skill or process integration, you need to start somewhere. Identify one of the areas within Audience Experience and focus on that before moving on to another element.
2. **Create a script** - even if scripting out verbatim what you are going to say for a session is not a common practice for you, when you start utilizing the processes in this section, it can help to create a script for the steps of the process you're working on. For instance, with the Activity Cycle, in your guide/notes, write out what you will say for each step of the process. This can give you something to lean on when you're in front of an audience.
3. **Give yourself grace** - it will feel clunky at first when incorporating these experience processes and you'll miss the mark at times. Don't beat yourself up. I've seen individuals completely lose focus during their session when they miss a step in a process, and it has a negative impact on the remaining portion of the session. If you know you miss a step, take a mental note, and move on.

I have seen countless presenters and facilitators struggle with these processes, and those that keep working are the ones that create the "muscle memory" faster which then feeds their confidence and the exceptional experiences become more common.

III

Success & Responsibility

9

Delivery Success

There are a multitude of books, videos, podcasts, articles, etc. based around the concept of success. All of these drive a great deal of value. Heck, I own a number of these types of books. Personally, when I read books like this, I know full well that 100% of the concepts may not apply to me. Yet I continue to consume them hoping to find a gem of knowledge that I can polish and make my own.

One of the most common themes of success books is defining how do you know when you're successful. Although there are perspectives that say you know you're successful, and I agree with that premise as it pertains to the various elements or roles we play in life (e.g. father, friend, leader). It is also imperative to realize that there should also be ways to score points that aid in our ability to reaffirm our levels of success.

Various check points or success markers for me along my journey have been when I got my first perfect score for facilitator ratings on a survey, getting master-certified in my first trainer certification program, being on stage in front of 2,000+ people.

My success markers grew over time.

When we think about our ability to create exceptional experiences for audiences, we need to know how to gauge our level of success.

I want to provide you with different ways you can gauge your progress as you are applying the various skills throughout this book. You may not use all of them every time you deliver a session, yet having these in your toolbox will help provide insights into gauging the success of your session.

"Light Bulb" Moments

These are the moments when you can see the audience gets it. This is a common pursuit angle for facilitators and presenters. It is something that will feed the excitement of even the most tenured presenters and facilitators.

The best way to watch for "light bulb" moments are the visible head nods. A certain level of relief that falls upon the faces of the audience. Relaxed muscles that transition to smiles and even raised eyebrows.

In some cases, audience members will share with you how they finally get it or defining how it makes sense after struggling with a concept.

Survey Scores

Surveys are commonly utilized post-session to gauge audience reactions. They have also lovingly been referred to as "Smile Sheets." These can get dismissed or overlooked at times depending on focus of the session, but this can be a great indicator for you as the one delivering the session if the audience enjoyed the experience.

These ratings or scores are insightful. Some of the most common are on a 5-point scale or in some situations survey questions for facilitators can be setup like a Net Promoter score.

If you decide to utilize a 5-point scale for a survey question, it is a great way to obtain straightforward feedback on the reactions of how you delivered the session. A couple sample versions of this type of survey question could be:

- How would you rate the presenter (5-highest; 1-lowest)?
- How would you rate the experience the facilitator created during your session (5-highest; 1-lowest)?

A Presenter/Facilitator Promoter Score can be slightly more complicated than a basic 5-point survey due to the additional rigor that goes into calculating the score. The promoter scoring is on a 10-point scale. Scores of 9 or 10 are classified as Promoters. Anything that is scored a 7 or 8 are classified as neutral responses. Then anything 6 and below are classified as Detractors.

To calculate a Promoter Score, you will add up the number of responses in each category (Promoters, Neutral, Detractors), then you will subtract the number of Detractors from the total number of Promoters. The remaining number of Promoters gives you the Promoter score.

For instance, if you have 100 responses, and you 10 Detractor responses, 20 Neutral responses, and 70 Promoter responses, you will subtract the 10 Detractors from the 70 Promoters, leaving you with a Promoter score of 60.

Simple formula: (Number of Promoters-Number of Detractors)/(Number of Respondents) x 100.

Here is a sample promoter score question: On a scale from 0-10, how likely are you to recommend the facilitator/presenter to a friend or colleague?

Either option can provide valuable insight for you as a presenter/facilitator when gauging the reactions to the experience you provide for your audiences.

If you are going to utilize a survey, it is also helpful to include a free response option for your audience. These are the question lines in a survey where audiences can add commentary about the experience. The anecdotal commentary that is added can provide valuable insight into why attendees scored the way they did. It can also provide insight into what may have resonated the most with the audience.

Application

The best sessions have action for the audience to apply. Within the learning industry, there are a lot of various philosophies to measure application (e.g. Kirkpatrick model). We won't dive deeply into these various avenues and theories, yet they can valuable if you need to have measurables to look at the success of your content.

For general purposes, hearing from audience members on how they applied their learnings from your session is powerful. These are great to capture for testimonials for your session(s).

If they take the time to share, whether in conversation or survey, the impact it had on their performance, this can demonstrate the impact your session had on your audience. Then you know you've impacted individuals. These impacts could be in job performance, personal growth, career advancement, etc.

If you decide to utilize a survey and you want to include a question around application, you can approach it two different ways. You can utilize a potential application impact question on a survey that is delivered immediately after your session. The other option is to deliver a survey after a prescribed period has passed (e.g. 60 days). The latter option will be determined by the measurement strategy set up prior to your session. This is also something that is seen most for training classes, not as often for presentations.

Here are some sample questions of each:

1. (Survey right after session) On a scale from 1-10, how likely are you to apply what you learned in the session?
2. (Survey sent after a prescribed time) After applying what you learned from _____, what results have you seen?

- Applied the knowledge and had concrete worthwhile results.
- Applied the knowledge but haven't seen any measurable results.
- Haven't applied the knowledge.

One thing to mention, the scale for your scoring can be adjusted (e.g. 5-point scale, 7-point scale), it is based on preference and the type of data insights you'd like to obtain. Similarly, the application with results type of response can be adjusted to meet the needs of your particular session.

These types of surveys can be valuable to help give you data points to demonstrate the level of success of the session you deliver.

Author note: In this application section, this is intended to provide a basic starting point if you've never utilized surveys or looking for a simple way to capture application insights. There is a lot of research on measuring learning and presentation impact (most notably: Kirkpatrick, Brinkerhoff, Phillips). I'd encourage you to explore more on this topic if you find it interesting.

Conversations

After you've wrapped up your session, attendees may come up to you afterwards. I mean, let's be honest, when you deliver an exceptional experience, you're operating at "Rock Star" level.

This engagement is powerful. Having audience members wanting to come talk to you after your session is wonderful. You can learn a ton from these conversations. Depending on the session, attendees may prefer to share personal connections to your content or something that resonated with them. When I've been at conferences and I've attended sessions, I will take the time to meet the speaker, if possible, because if they delivered an exceptional session, I want to take the time to let them know. They have always been appreciative of the feedback, and I've developed friendships with these speakers because of it. When you find yourself in the shoes of completing a session, I encourage you to make the time to meet with your audience. Getting the feedback in the moment is amazing.

Having conversations about your session also allows you to hear the questions that may be lingering for attendees. This can help with updating an upcoming session on a similar topic.

Unwavering Loyalty

As you become more seasoned and you deliver more session, you will start build more notoriety. With the level of popularity, you will start to create a bit of a following. Whether you are working with a company or work for yourself, you will become more recognizable. By becoming more recognizable for the experiences you create, you will start see a lot of familiar faces in your sessions. People will want to attend your sessions because YOU are delivering it. That is what I deem as unwavering loyalty.

This is the level of impact that gets overlooked at times, and it is a huge confidence boost.

Unwavering loyalty is the perspective that attendees, or past attendees, mention, "I don't know what your topic is, but if you're delivering it, I know it will be good." This is the ultimate compliment, especially if it is a referral. Where someone attends then mentions a friend of theirs told them they had to attend your session.

During my time at a financial institution, a colleague and I were asked to create sessions for their annual client conferences. The conference was around the solutions this group provided around Compliance related topics. This type of audience can be tough considering our subject matter was focused mainly on soft skills.

During our 2nd year, we had a few clients make it a point to attend our session and even more so, sit in the front. Not only were they wonderful people but when they shared, they enjoyed the session so much the previous year, they made it a point to come to another.

To this day, it is one of the best compliments I've ever received as a presenter or facilitator.

By pursuing unwavering loyalty through the experiences you create, you will make valuable connections and you will see your brand as an exceptional presenter or facilitator continue to grow.

Identifying the success of your sessions is a powerful way to ensure you're meeting the needs of your audience, and the content is resonating with them. Understanding your Delivery Success is a great way to boost your confidence and to know where you need to enhance areas in your delivery to continue to evolve.

10

Transferable Skills

Being talented at facilitating or presenting a session to an audience is a skill that should go beyond a classroom or stage.

Now do me a favor and go back and read that sentence again.

What word stood out to you?

SHOULD.

Hoping that was the word that stood out to you. And now that you've gone back to that sentence again and reread it after I pointed it out (be honest, you know you did), it likely drove an odd reaction from you.

You may ask, "Why?"

You may think, "Duh!"

You may have had the reaction of, "Hell no!"

Whatever your reaction was, it is important to understand the skills covered in this book are transferrable to any environment in which you are communicating verbally.

Far too many times I have seen dynamic speakers that "pull up lame" in every other environment when they are engaging with other humans.

Trust me, I get the fact that there are very talented presenters and facilitators that are natural introverts and don't need to be the life of the party. I am one of them. My natural state is one of observation and listening.

The difference is that "switch" we talked about earlier that gets flipped when it's time to be in front of an audience should have a dimmer control to it, and when it is time to communicate, it still gets flipped to the "on" position. The purpose for having a bit of a dimmer switch is if you are in a 1-on-1, you may not go through your full Prep Sequence, but you should still tap into your honed skills.

Let's say you are getting ready to have a 1-on-1 with your boss, you will want an agenda, you likely have an objective or two you want to achieve from the meeting, you want to show up with presence, make eye contact, be present, minimize nervous habits, and tackle questions appropriately. Even with these few examples, you are leveling up the interaction. This can bode well for you, especially if you aspire of eventually taking over for your boss one day.

The ability to effectively communicate is a powerful tool in any setting. By shifting your mindset that these skills can be honed in various setting is a great way to practice. Dedicating time to refine the skill-set is very valuable.

Find ways to practice. It could be in a team meeting, giving a small presentation, 1:1s, or even at the drive thru.

Take a moment and think about 2-3 "tools" that stood out to you from this book.

Now write down at least one way each of those skills could be applied into a setting outside of a presentation or facilitated class.

Here are a few examples:

a. Presence during a networking event

- Are you standing confidently?
- Are you articulating clearly?
- Are you building rapport?

b. Strong Opening for a meeting

- Did you establish the WIIFM (e.g. purpose of the meeting)?
- Did you review the agenda?
- Did you review the objectives (e.g. goals/outcomes of the meeting)?

c. Clear communication at the drive thru

- Are you enunciating the words clearly?
- Are you connecting/building rapport with the worker?
- Did you smile?

These examples are outlined to get you thinking clearly that the skills reviewed in this book should be utilized at as many places as possible, not just in a structured event (presentation or class).

This has been a common misconception for trainers/presenters I have witnessed that they can be very dynamic in front of an audience, but don't utilize their skills when interacting with other humans. Any interaction with others humans is still an audience.

Virtual Delivery

A very interesting shift was thrust upon the profession of facilitating and presenting in March 2020. For those that lived through that, they are very familiar with what occurred at that time. The global pandemic (COVID) that essentially paralyzed the world and accelerated a shift that was slowly building on the horizon. That was the skill-set of facilitating classes and delivering presentations on virtual platforms like Zoom or Webex. Platforms such as those were already heavily utilized at that time for meetings yet hadn't fully been adopted into mainstream utilization for presenting and facilitating.

The pandemic was a lightning bolt that jolted the profession that forced many facilitators and presenters to pivot quickly.

In March of 2020, I was leading a learning organization and we had been doing some virtual classes, but the bulk of our sessions were in-person. When the world began to shut down, we were forced to convert our classes from 90/10 split of in-person to virtual to 100% virtual within a week.

The great news is we were able to lean on the expertise we had within the team that had been leading virtual sessions to quickly upskill the rest of the team that hadn't been accustomed to delivering sessions virtually.

I mention this because not only was this a pivotal time for facilitators and presenters but because it highlighted that gap in mindset on the skills that transfer from in-person to virtual sessions.

Delivering a session virtually has become more common and it created a very scalable solution for mass communication that minimizes costs of travel (e.g. bringing attendees together from various locations). When prior to that, there was still a common perspective that if a session is to be effective it needs to be in-person. While I still believe there is immense value with in-person sessions, which allows for enhanced connection between humans, exceptional experiences can be created virtually.

There are many wonderful books on the art of virtual delivery. They focus on quality engagement when an audience is not in the same location. I have had success delivering sessions virtually, but I wouldn't classify myself as an expert in this space. I'd encourage you to check out the work from an experts in virtual delivery. Kassy LaBorie is a wonderful example. She is an expert and is a pioneer that has had an immense amount of success delivering sessions virtually and has coached countless presenters and facilitators on this art form. Experts, such as Kassie, can provide quality guidance around the art of virtual facilitation.

For our purposes here, I wanted to aid in the understanding of truly what are some of the transferable skills that can enhance your ability if you are delivering a session virtually.

Here are some basic skills that transfer to the virtual world:

- Eye contact
- Facial Expressions
- Hands
- Utilize your Preparation Sequence
- Tackling Questions

Eye Contact

When delivering a session, your audience wants to feel you are truly communicating with them. This is very hard to create that experience when people are staring down your ear canal. Too many times when attending anything virtually (e.g. meetings) people are too worried about what is comfortable for them, they feel they need to see the people they are talking to, so they stare at the window with the images of others in the virtual room. When those images are away from the camera, the audience is looking at the side of the face of the person speaking. As a presenter or facilitator, it is important to maintain focus on creating an exceptional experience. This starts with looking at the camera when talking. You want the audience members to feel you are talking directly to them.

> *"But what if I can't see the people within the platform window? I need to be able to see them."*

This is a common rebuke to the point of looking down the barrel of the camera. I remind those that have that level of worry, that it is not about what is most comfortable for you, it is in the best interest for your audience. To assist with combating that, have your camera at your eye level, then on the screen, place the platform window as close to the camera lens as possible. Reduce the window size and place it as close to the camera (e.g. just under the camera). This then minimizes your eye deviation when you need to glance at the chat pane or gauge reactions. In addition, this also allows you to tap into your peripheral vision to monitor changes within the window (e.g. hand raised).

Facial Expressions

Demonstrating a level of expression with your face is one of your most valuable assets in the virtual space. Which should make sense since your audience is unable to read the rest of your body language. What shows up on your face is the main way for your virtual audience to interpret your non-verbals.

This may mean leaning more into your facial warm-up activities before a virtual session to keep the muscles in your face more pliable and ready for showtime.

Hands

If you naturally talk with your hands, raise your hand. Yes, I know that may have felt weird raising your hand while you are reading this, but thank you for playing along.

This is a common question I will ask my audiences for training/presentation skills sessions. The majority of the folks I've worked with will raise their hands.

Here's the interesting part, with many individuals having a natural proclivity to talk with their hands, it has always baffled me that once they step into the virtual ring, hand usage goes down.

When you are in the virtual space environment, it is important to continue to utilize your hand gestures. Like what we covered earlier in the book, utilizing your hands and speaking naturally aids in your ability to demonstrate authenticity.

Even though your audience only sees a small window of your image in the virtual space, it is a great best practice to ensure your virtual audience can see your hands. It is a natural reaction for people in general that if they can see your hands, they will trust you more (if you want to nerd-out and learn more about why that occurs, check out Vanessa Van Edwards' research).

This may mean you need to back up a little from your camera, so your audience sees more of you or you bring your hands up closer to shoulder level.

One of the most engaging virtual facilitators I've ever seen is a former colleague of mine. Adam had an amazing ability to connect with his virtual audience and it took me awhile to figure it out. Yes, he is an amazing facilitator and a great person, but one of his strongest attributes when he's delivering virtually is he keeps his hands close to shoulder level. This keeps them visible a large portion of the time, which aids in his ability to build trust with his audiences.

Utilize your Preparation Sequence

You've built up your sequence and you know what you need to be optimized for your sessions, don't overlook incorporating your sequence just because you're stepping into the virtual arena.

Treat this engagement like any other session you may deliver. Put yourself into the right frame of mind and treat it like any other experience that you want to make exceptional.

Tackling Questions

You've built the muscle memory to ensure questions are addressed accordingly when interacting with other humans. Just like taking the time to practice at your favorite fast food establishment's drive-thru, follow the process in the virtual environment.

This even applies to questions that come in through the chat pane of the virtual platform.

When a question comes in, acknowledge the question by saying the person's name.

Here is an example on how I would set up the Tackling Questions process for a question that comes in through the chat:

> "Tammy... I see you asked a question around ideal ways to keep learners engaged in the virtual environment. Would you mind coming off mute

and expanding on your question for me? I want to make sure I hit the mark for you."

Notice I incorporated the Listen and Recap step all at once. I also added the brief pause to allow Tammy to know I am speaking to her directly so she can collect her thoughts before responding. Did you catch the virtual ninja trick I deployed as well?

By asking for clarity on the question, I am now getting her to come off mute which drives more dialogue with the audience. This is valuable in the virtual space as it is easy for audience members to "hide" their true engagement via chat.

The important thing to keep in mind, that regardless of the situation, the skills and behaviors reviewed in this book are transferable into any type of situation.

11

Grow, Pursue, Pass on

Growing Your Skills

The ability to build, grow, refine, hone a set of skills takes an insane amount of time. When it comes to the ability to be a great facilitator or presenter, it is no different. The most eye-glaringly difference is the fact you have an audience as you work on your skills. The audience could be a handful, or it could be thousands. I believe this is why individuals are reluctant to work on the skills.

I'll admit it is nerve-racking. Because with any new skill, there are going to be times when things don't go as planned and as much as we would love to mask those situations, audiences see it.

I have two vivid memories when the wheels completely came off for me when I was in front of an audience. There were two people, in which I can still picture their faces and remember their names, because in the moment, they helped me get through it.

The first one was when I was in high school in Carmel, IN and I was in a public speaking class my senior year. In this class, we learned all the various types of public speaking (e.g. debate, speeches). We were supposed to deliver a speech on this day and while I was delivering my 7-minute speech, I got completely lost and started fumbling around. I remember glancing up and I made eye contact with a girl in the class, Meredith. It was helpful because when I made eye contact with her, she gave me a smile. Not a "I'm laughing at you" smile, but it was one of those supportive "You got this" smiles. Now it didn't hurt that I liked her, and she was easy on the eyes, but in the moment that is what I needed to get back on track.

The other instance was when I was delivering my first trainer certification course by myself. I got so lost in the Discussions module, I just stopped talking. I was scrambling through my notes while the thought was racing through my mind, "how in the hell am I going to get myself out of this?" Thankfully I happen to be standing nearby a very sweet lady (Cheryl) who was attending the class and she whispered, "It's ok, you got this." This allowed me to take a breath, relax, and get back on track.

I mention both of those instances to remind you that as worrisome as it is to stumble in front of an audience as you are working on your craft to be exceptional in front of an audience, the majority of the time, your audiences can and will be supportive. When those moments arise, those simple reaffirming expressions will help you get through those dreaded moments.

As you continue to grow your skills, there are three things that can be valuable to review, assess, and improve:

1. Mental Checklists
2. Observations
3. Study Game Film

Mental Checklists

As you go through a session, you will inevitably have a checklist of things always running through your mind, even while you're in front of the audience. There are times when there are multiple checklists running through your mind at a time. The checklist that is tactic related (e.g. achieving all the elements of your opening, tackling questions appropriately). Another checklist may be related to the content (e.g. executing an activity correctly, staying on time with the agenda).

It is ok to have these mental checklists running, however be careful it doesn't derail you while in front of an audience. Derailment can occur when you miss a step of a tactic process, which occurred in my first trainer certification example. As soon as your brain sets off your "you screwed that up" alarm, you have to remain focused to keep moving forward.

To help aid in your ability to minimize your opportunity for derailment, set a plan for your mental checklist. This could potentially be part of your Prep Sequence. Keep in mind, this would be different from any type of preparation checklist that I've seen other presenters or facilitators use. Since you will already have a mental manifest running in your brain while in front of your audience, you might as well control it as best you can.

Your planned Mental Checklist should be simple. Know going into your session what the top things you want to have running in your brain during your session.

Depending on what you may be working on or priorities for the session, your Mental Checklist could be: Tackle Questions & End on Time.

If these two things are running through my mind during the session, I am being extra vigilant on achieving the each of the steps to address questions appropriately and I am keeping an eye on the time. This can help keep you focused without getting too overwhelmed with the number of things that are constantly being balanced in your brain during a session.

A great way to help set focus for your mental checklist is knowing what you should be working on, and you can obtain that insight through observations.

Observations

Obtaining feedback from others, especially those that understand the facilitation and presentation skill-set, is valuable. If you work within a company and you are on a team with other professionals doing a similar role (e.g. corporate training teams), you will likely be observed by your boss. This is usually an indicator that leaders within a training organization will use to measure performance. Which means there is usually a score of some kind.

However, observations don't always have to be formal. I've seen immense value come from peer observations. If you can leverage peer observations, two things occur. It is a great way to get more feedback and an even better way to share best practices between colleagues. I've always enjoyed not only conducting peer observations, but I love getting peer feedback. When you get peer feedback, it will almost always come with a new way of looking at how to approach a particular situation. With peer feedback, it is usually anecdotal feedback.

There is also a third type of feedback that you can receive and that is content related feedback. This type of feedback is helpful to hear from someone that is very familiar with the content you are covering. It can help to hear ideas of how to convey certain concepts differently to help enhance the audiences understanding of the subject matter.

If you schedule time for someone to observe you, there a few things to remember:

- You may not agree with all the feedback, which is ok. Accept it anyway. View feedback as a gift and no matter what try to find something that you can add to your toolbox to make you better.
- Try to focus the observation. This is helpful with peer observations. If a peer is planning to sit in on your session, let them know the top couple things you are working on and ask that they provide feedback in those areas, yet welcome any other insights they offer.
- Minimize the volume of observations. The goal with observations is to identify successes and opportunities in your skill-set so you can start working on improving them. It is way too difficult to apply feedback if you are getting observations done at a high volume. If you are getting observation feedback daily, or even once a week, it can be hard to apply all that feedback within those windows of time. Set a cadence that works for you, even if that means having a conversation with those doing the observations requesting to back off the volume so you have time to apply the feedback and improve.

Pro Tip: *When presenting or facilitating a session and an observer is in the room, try not to focus on them. It works best to ignore they are even there. If you focus on the observer, it will inevitably detract from creating the best possible audience experience.*

Not everyone will have the luxury to have a consistent stream of observations for their sessions. Which is why, watching yourself can be valuable.

Watch Game Film

The concept of "Watch Game Film" is one that is common in sports, especially in football. A team will play a game then they will go back and comb over every ounce of the game to see how the team performed. They will assess the execution against the game plan. They will rewind a video hundreds of times to see if there were missed assignments. Identify what plays broke down and why. Then they will take these video breakdowns back to the team to coach them up to eliminate mistakes and celebrate successes.

This same concept is valuable even when you're in front of an audience. You can go back to assess all the granular things covered in this book to critique what worked and what did not. The tough part is most individuals do not like to see themselves on video.

It is a common innate trait amongst humans to not want to see themselves on video. There are some people that don't even like to see pictures of themselves. The reason is we are hyper-critical of ourselves. We critique how we look, faces we make, how we act, how we're dressed... the list can go on.

However, there is a great deal of power to use that critical review to your advantage. Watching your game film can be a great way to accelerate your skill-set when you're in front of an audience. If you are able to record a presentation or class that you are leading, you can quickly identify your gaps.

Although it is easy to focus solely on the "negatives" that appear to us, yet it is important to focus on what went well. Did you effectively tell a story? Did you make great eye contact? Was there solid laughter at your intended humor? Did you successfully deliver an impactful opening or power closing?

Similar to football coaches who want to assess what needs to be fixed, they also need to celebrate the successes to let the team know where they did something well. When you watch your game film, focus on the opportunities so you can improve, but don't lose sight of things that went well. This is the exact reason when deliver feedback after an observation, I will always start with, "What went well?"

There may be situations when you may not have recording capabilities. You still have your Mental Checklist, but another avenue that helps is to study the greats.

One area that has helped me tremendously is to be a student of the game. I enjoy watching great presenters and facilitators. I have watched many hours of speeches or recordings because I have a great appreciation for the art form and love seeing it in action at a mastery level. By studying game film of others, especially the greats, I can identify elements that I may be able to incorporate into my style.

Here are some examples:

- Tony Robbins - sustained energy; emotional range
- Simon Sinek - simplicity of delivery; even paced story telling
- Dan Pink - effective word usage; engaging voice tambor

These three gentlemen have hours upon hours of video content available and in my humble opinion are on my "Mount Rushmore" of great orators of our time.

Take a moment to reflect back on presenters or facilitators you've seen. Who would be on your "Mount Rushmore" of greats?

Being a student of the game can be a blessing and curse. I have grown to have such an affinity for this art form, it is hard not to get distracted by solely focusing on the delivery of a session. If I attend a class or a presentation, I get so wrapped up in observing the presenter/trainer that I forget to engage in the content. Yes, I have been caught off guard focusing on the delivery then we are put into an activity and I have had no idea what we are supposed to be doing because I was locked into the delivery.

This happens with excellent and poor presenters and facilitators. If I am attending a session that is delivered exceptionally well, I get caught up jotting down notes about why it was so good or ideas to enhance my skill-set. Similarly, if the session is delivered poorly, I struggle to remain focused and immediately start looking for an escape hatch out of the room. I know it's awful, but it can be very distracting for me.

As you become a student of the game, I will share a helpful tip that I learned especially if you become locked in on the delivery and need to focus on the content. Find a way to turn-off the delivery focused switch. Easier said than done, but I must tell myself I can't focus on the delivery as I want to soak in the subject matter. It is a bit of a mindset shift, but it can certainly help as you become more of a student of the game.

Pursue Unattainable Perfection

> *"Mastery is a process, not a destination."* - Bill Walsh

The skill of presenting and facilitating is an evolving skill-set. No matter how polished you are or how many times you've delivered a session, there is always a new dynamic that presents itself. It could be the size of an audience. It could be utilizing a new technology. It could be bad habit that reappears. It could be you are asked to deliver a session in an old bank vault (yes, that happened to me). Whatever the situation, it is something that always seems to evolve and just when you think you've seen or done it all, you can still be surprised.

There have been many times where I have demonstrated a particular skill or behavior at a very high level, yet unfortunately, I was baffled when I regressed. At least for me, it showed up out of nowhere.

There was an instance when I felt very comfortable with the removal of filler words (uh/um). I had worked on my pacing and improving my preparation with the content so I wouldn't searching for what to say next. Then came the day when I realized filler words did not hold exclusive rights to "uh & um."

Apparently, filler words filed some sort of patent on all language. I learned the hard way that multi-syllabic words are included in the strangle hold that filler words have on all language.

After working so hard to alleviate "uh's and um's" my confidence was high going into a session. Unbeknownst to me, in a session in which I was being observed I added "absolutely" into my repetitive vernacular. During a module, it was counted that I said "absolutely" 27 times within a two-hour timeframe. Yikes!!! It had become my crutch word to acknowledge any contribution from the learners during that module.

It is art form is one that needs to be consistently refined and by us being humans, we change.

If you are new to the profession, I mention this because it is not something I want you to walk away discouraged. It is more to level set the expectation that refinement takes time, and it takes a dedicated pursuit toward perfection that aid in your growth.

One area that helped me was to focus on continuous growth and celebrating even the littlest of victories.

When starting out, it can be valuable to establish various milestones for sustained growth.

Milestone examples:

- Deliver a session without vomiting beforehand
- Be engaging enough that learners willingly participate
- Understand subject matter well enough to be less dependent on guides/script

- Achieve >95% survey rating on your session
- Achieve any type of high level or "Master" certification in facilitation/training/presenting
- Deliver a presentation at a conference

These may not be milestones for everyone, yet they can allow for folks new to the craft to strive toward growth while celebrating along the way.

Pursuing perfection is my bar. I know it cannot be achieved. Knowing the level of perfection is unattainable, that is what also fuels my relentless pursuit. Pursuing perfection may not be your ultimate end goal. You may be looking to pick up some skills so you can deliver a 15-minute session during a team meeting without the violent urge to throw up. Whatever standard you pursue, the key is to identify it and not give up.

In high school, I had classes where we were asked to speak in front of our classmates. I would get nervous, it's high school after all, yet always felt comfortable and confident. Then when I started college and took the required freshman public speaking class which in turn ultimately opened the door of opportunity to get my degree in Speech Communications, my love for the art form began to blossom.

Even with the number of classes I attended during my school years, it was not until I met Jeff Moore, that I realized how far I had to go to be great.

With thousands of presenters and facilitators that I have seen in classes I've attended, observed, coached, or mentored, Jeff Moore is hands down the best facilitator I have ever seen. He set the bar I pursue daily.

Prior to attending my first class with Jeff, which was a trainer certification class, a colleague of mine told me, "Really watch what he does, every single thing he teaches during the class, he is demonstrating it." It didn't make sense in that moment, but once I saw it in action, I knew I was watching greatness.

His mastery of the art form is off the charts. He could get a group of people thinking and moving in unison toward a goal so seamlessly. No matter the situation, he would never miss a step. The thing that I always have admired is his almost instant ability to connect with his audiences. I continue to learn from him even in our 20 years of friendship.

I mention Jeff because as you hone your skills, I challenge you to find your performance bar, or your "Jeff," that you can pursue. It will keep that fire burning inside you which in turn prevents complacency.

Pass On

We all possess the ability to communicate effectively. The better we can become, the more we can thrive, both personally and professionally. Growing that skill-set is something that should start early in life.

Kids need to know how to express themselves effectively. Whether it is communicating how they are feeling, engaging with teachers/adults, and even simply making friends.

Each generation is different. Priorities changes. Technology changes. The one thing that is true is we are still humans. Our primary mode of communication is verbally. It is our responsibility to help foster this skill-set to equip our future generations to find their voice. Whether you have kids of your own or not, kids are impressionable. It starts with our ability to demonstrate the skill-set we've honed.

We must be able to demonstrate the ability to be successful in articulating our thoughts by using our voice. Young kids may not realize what they are seeing, but it remains with them when they see effective communication.

If kids see us moving beyond our fears of speaking in front of an audience, they now have a great example of overcoming their own fears. Which in turn boosts their confidence.

What I have done to start my boys down this path is instead of sending thank you cards after their birthday parties; they create Thank You videos. I talk through what they feel they should say, sometimes there is coaching to ensure they say thank you, then I record them. Those videos are sent to the parents of the friends. Aside from making sure they say thank you for the specific gift they receive (I don't want it to feel generic with one video for everyone), I let them add whatever comes to mind. This has led to some hilarious clips. Nothing screams authentic messaging from a four-year-old that ends a thank you video with "I love you," a big tiger roar, and sprinting out of frame.

My intent is to build the skill-set over time. The value of teaching kids at a young age to be comfortable effectively communicating to an audience is it creates future leaders. Regardless of the direction they take their profession, it is a skill-set that will serve them well.

Starting points for kids:

- Shaking hands while making eye contact
- Telling stories
- Send video recordings for "thank you" messages
- Read out loud, practice cadence, especially around punctuation

By investing your valuable time to reading this book, you are committing to honing your craft as a facilitator or presenter. This skill-set comes with responsibilities. We must continue to find ways to grow our skills. The drive to grow our skills and hone our craft is fueled by our pursuit of being masters of those skills. That drive to become better and getting to a place where we consistently demonstrating a level of mastery, we must prepare future generations to embrace the power that comes from moving an audience.

Are you willing to accept the responsibilities with this art form?

12

Wrap Up

Throughout this book, there has been a number of concepts, perspectives, processes, and random stories from a career that started by stumbling into it and turned into an obsession. My purpose for writing this book was to equip any presenter or facilitator with the tools necessary to build confidence to successfully deliver any type of session.

The four key categories to achieve delivery success are: Authenticity, Confidence, Preparation, and Audience Experience.

Authenticity dove into movement, voice, word choice, gestures, and eye contact so you can always show up as your true self.

Confidence explored how presence, humor, being present, nervous habits, and appearance can make you unflappable.

Preparation took the unique journey through self, refocus your mind, materials, technology, room set-up, and the preparation sequence to ensure you are ready for any scenario.

Audience Experience delved into the focus on experience, impactful openings, activity cycle, question types, tackling questions, power closings, and reading

WRAP UP

the room to tactically enhance what your audiences experience.

All with the intent to ensure every session you deliver for your audiences is exceptional.

What I would like you to do now is take 5-10 minutes to look back through the book or notes you've taken. Then write down separately, the top 1-2 items you want to immediately begin applying in one of your upcoming sessions.

If you want to amplify your commitment to the application of these top 1-2 items, I challenge you to share these items. This could be sharing with colleagues, your significant other, or even posting it on social media (#DSYDB). Accepting this challenge will aid in your personal accountability to the top items you've identified.

As mentioned previously, the art of facilitating and presenting is an ever-evolving skill-set and in order to demonstrate mastery, it takes a commitment to the craft. Which is why I love this quote from Aristotle:

> "To be excellent we cannot simply think or feel excellent, we must act excellently."

Thank you dedicating your time to read this book. Your time is valuable, and I feel if you can hone at least your top takeaways from this book, you will have received a return on this investment and you will avoid showing your duck butt.

Appendix

Cheat Codes

The ability to present and facilitate stretches across an array of situations and circumstances since it is communication with other humans. Regardless of why you picked up this book or where you are in your journey in refining your skills with this art form, here are some Cheat Codes.

These Cheat Codes are targeted areas that you can focus on depending on where you are in your journey or want to refine a particular area. This will allow you the opportunity to focus your skill development and when those become better refined and you want to enhance another area, you can come back and grab new areas to enhance.

Cheat Code #1 – Just starting your journey		
Authenticity	Voice	These elements allow you to focus on the basics to get you started. Keeping it simple.
Authenticity	Eye Contact	
Confidence	Being Present	
Preparation	Materials	

APPENDIX

Cheat Code #2 – Personal confidence booster		
Authenticity	Voice	
Confidence	Being Present	These elements intended to reflect internally and help boost your internal confidence which will portray stronger confidence to your audience.
Confidence	Presence	
Confidence	Appearance	
Preparation	Self	
Preparation	Refocus Your Mind	

Cheat Code #3 – Level up		
Authenticity	Movement	
Authenticity	Gestures	
Confidence	Nervous Habits	These elements are intended to go beyond the basics when you've demonstrated a strong understanding of the basics.
Confidence	Presence	
Preparation	Self	
Preparation	Prep Sequence	
Audience Exp.	Focus on Experience	
Audience Exp.	Question Types	

Cheat Code #4 – Senior Level		
Confidence	Presence	
Authenticity	Humor	
Prepatation	Self	These elements are designed to enhance the skills of those that have attained a higher-level facilitator position and want to continue to grow their skills.
Preparation	Refocus Your Mind	
Audience Exp	Focus on Experience	
Audience Exp	Impactful Openings	
Audience Exp.	Tackling Questions	
Audience Exp.	Power Closings	

Cheat Code #5 – Presentation Focus

Category	Element	Description
Authenticity	Voice	
Authenticity	Word Choice	
Confidence	Nervous Habits	
Confidence	Presence	These elements are intended to go beyond the basics when you've demonstrated a strong understanding of the basics.
Preparation	Self	
Preparation	Prep Sequence	
Audience Exp.	Focus on Experience	
Audience Exp.	Impactful Openings	
Audience Exp.	Powerful Closings	

Cheat Code #6 – Executive Presence

Category	Element	Description
Authenticity	Voice	
Authenticity	Eye Contact	
Confidence	Presence	
Confidence	Nervous Habits	These elements are focused on enhancing the skills when presenting in front of an executive audience.
Preparation	Self	
Preparation	Refocus Your Mind	
Audience Exp.	Focus on Experience	
Audience Exp.	Tackling Questions	
Audience Exp.	Reading the Room	

Cheat Code #7 – Ultimate Ninja Skills

Category	Element	Description
Confidence	Being Present	
Preparation	Self	
Preparation	Prep Sequence	
Preparation	Refocus Your Mind	These elements are the ultimate package that will move any presenter/facilitator from good to great.
Audience Exp.	Impactful Openings	
Audience Exp.	Activity Cycle	
Audience Exp.	Tackling Questions	
Audience Exp.	Power Closings	

www.ingramcontent.com/pod-product-compliance
Lightning Source LLC
Chambersburg PA
CBHW060455030426
42337CB00015B/1605